THOUGHT CATALOG BOOKS

A Thousand New Beginnings

A Thousand New Beginnings

Tales of Solo Female Travel Through Southeast Asia

KRISTIN ADDIS

Thought Catalog Books

Brooklyn, NY

THOUGHT CATALOG BOOKS

Copyright © 2016 by Kristin Addis

All rights reserved. Published by Thought Catalog Books, a division of The Thought & Expression Co., Williamsburg, Brooklyn. Founded in 2010, Thought Catalog is a website and imprint dedicated to your ideas and stories. We publish fiction and non-fiction from emerging and established writers across all genres. For general information and submissions: manuscripts@thoughtcatalog.com.

First edition, 2016
ISBN 978-0692662885
10 9 8 7 6 5 4 3 2 1

Cover photography by © Kristin Addis

Foreword

It was April 4, 2013 in the late afternoon. I sat at my big IKEA desk in the corner of my room in Newport Beach, California. It was the very place I'd sat for the months of February and March when I did almost nothing but read travel blogs day in and day out. They helped me to realize that people who aren't trust fund babies can travel, too.

This wasn't the first time I'd done a flight search, stared at the screen, and hesitated. Just like all the other times, the possibility was very real that I'd get cold feet and close the search window again.

My fingers hovered over the keyboard. Could I really do it? As soon as I did, I knew that it would all be real. The chain reaction would start and the floodgates would open. I'd be standing right in the thick of it, learning how to swim.

I asked myself, "Are you really ready to buy the one-way ticket to Bangkok? Are you truly prepared for all of the things that it will mean?"

I had been contemplating a solo journey for the better part of a year at that point. I knew I needed to shake life up but I didn't feel ready to demolish the bridges behind me yet. I was worried I'd walk away from a chance at a good, stable life with a solid career as an investment banker and a four-year relationship with someone who I knew really loved me. I was afraid I'd never get those things again if I let go of them then and there. Out of fear, I held onto what was easy and familiar for years even though it was at odds with what my soul longed to do – I wanted to be free.

I also couldn't shake the feeling that something just wasn't right with my life at that point. I had felt it for far too long. I recall sitting on the beach with my now ex who would say, "I don't get it. Your life is perfect. You have a good job that most people would kill for and you live in paradise. If you can't be happy here I'm not sure if you can be happy anywhere."

Yet I knew he was wrong. I didn't want to stay in a situation where my dreams weren't supported and to oscillate between contentedness and frustration just because I was too scared to take a leap of faith, stuck in a pattern of desiring to go but never pulling the trigger.

All this passed through my mind as I contemplated buying that one-way ticket and the answer that night was finally, "Yes. I'm ready."

As if pushed by an invisible hand, I finally hit the purchase button and a wave of heat went through me. I hadn't told anyone about my desire to travel yet. I kept it secret because I didn't want anyone to talk me out of it until it was a done deal.

Well that night, it became real and I knew what I had to do. I had to let everyone know that I would be leaving fewer than six months later with nothing but a carry-on bag on my back and a dream in my heart, and that I didn't know when I'd be back.

The following is a series of excerpts from a blog that I started back then to chronicle the journey, plus many private things I wrote along the way but never posted. I published it in the way I would a private journal, as if talking to someone who couldn't talk back, but a companion nonetheless because as a solo traveler, it comforted me to have an outlet for my thoughts, even if nobody, at least at first, was listening.

The following is the story of an ordinary girl who set out to do something extraordinary – travel the world all by herself, and live to tell the tale.

Part 1

I Bought a One-Way Ticket to Bangkok

1

September 10, 2012

It's true. I bought a one-way ticket to Bangkok. I have absolutely no solid plans, and for once, I'm okay with that.

It sounds a little crazy to simply pack up and leave, I know. What makes a person walk away from a steady job, lovely beachside apartment, and a four-year relationship? All I can manage when asked this question is that I simply need to.

I need to do this.

All I have ever really wanted out of the world is to see the whole of it.

I spent the early part of my 20s as an investment banker. Life was so structured for so long, it was stifling. I couldn't breathe. My stress levels were at an all-time high, and frankly, I was suffering from depression. My life felt as grey as the walls of my cubicle. Each year blurred into the next. When I look back on the past four years, I can hardly separate one from the other.

I found myself questioning everything I had been conditioned to believe. I started to realize that "success" was subjective, and for me, it didn't mean owning things. I had worked my butt off in order to buy a purse, or a necklace, or a dress, only to realize that they brought me no joy. It didn't seem like this was the way life was supposed to work.

So I quit.

Then I bought a one-way ticket to the other side of the world. I chose Thailand because it's cheap and I have some Asia experience from when I moved to Taipei at age twenty-one to study Mandarin.

Next, I sold everything I owned in the span of one week so that I couldn't possibly change my mind.

I'm going alone, which freaks me out a little. I've never traveled long-term on my own. I have never even backpacked.

I've hardly ever even been single. It seems to me that I need this. If nothing else, just to get to know *me* a little better.

Back in my cubicle-dwelling days, nomadic women who wrote about their journeys and experiences online continuously inspired me. Seeing how many strong women were out there living out my dream made me realize it was a possibility for me, too.

I hatched the plan last year to take my savings and travel the world with it. I thought about what I was leaving behind: the guaranteed comforts and security of a home, a good job, and a relationship that was heading toward marriage. Not a day went by that I didn't feel the pain in my chest knowing that I was about to demolish all of those bridges. I felt guilty, but at the same time, I couldn't ignore the pull to explore the world.

I worried I'd have regrets for the rest of my life if I didn't take this chance. I didn't want to end up bitter.

So here I am, with nothing left but a carry-on backpack and a ticket in my hand.

I do hope you'll follow along. I promise to make it worth your while.

2

September 27, 2012

Day 1

1 AM at LAX: I was dropped off about an hour ago after needing a pep-talk to help me not feel stressed about this trip. Though I didn't cry this time (I did when I moved to Taiwan five years ago), I feel a good amount of fear of the unknown – mostly about landing in Bangkok and having no idea what to do next, coupled with fear of doing this alone.

An announcement comes over the loudspeaker: it's time to board. Thank goodness, because I'm exhausted.

6 AM in Taipei: After getting a full ten hours of sleep on the plane (even *I'm* surprised at my good sleep fortune), I wake up to a hot breakfast and finally feel calm and ready for what's next. I booked a window seat months ago knowing that it would be worth the thirteen hours shoved in a corner just for the chance to see Taiwan again as I landed.

Almost exactly five years ago, as a scared 21-year-old girl who was on her own for the first time, I arrived here with no idea of what kind of adventure laid before me. It's funny how life tends to come full circle.

Oddly enough, it looks different to me today than it did

back in 2008. Yet, as I exit the plane, a familiar and pacifying smell greets me: humidity mixed with wet concrete, beef noodles, and the perfume of the duty-free shops in the airport.

I wait at my gate in what must be a newly revamped terminal. It's shiny and pristine, lined with Gucci and Prada shops. Laying here in a reclined seat, enjoying the free Wi-Fi (I'm not even in a fancy lounge, this airport freaking rocks), and gathering my thoughts, my heart hurts a little to know that I'm only passing through what was once my home. It is becoming more and more clear to me that I'll have to return to this beautiful island in the very near future.

11 AM in Bangkok: I land and start following the masses out of the terminal. Bangkok Airport is huge and bustling. I wander around a bit like a lost puppy trying to figure out if I need to purchase a visa or not. I decide to just try for immigration and find that it was the right choice. An unsmiling female agent hands my passport back to me with permission to stay for thirty days, and I make my way to the taxi station.

I have nothing booked and no idea what exactly to do next. So, I ask the taxi driver to take me to Khao San Road – a place I've heard is a backpacker's haven.

I settle in my seat and happily watch out the window at the gridlock and the heat vapor rising up from the asphalt. Taxis of all colors pass me by from classic yellow, to green, to Barbie pink.

It's nice to be in Asia again. I missed this chaos.

1 PM Khao San Road: Waving off the aggressive tuk-tuk drivers, I take a right and find a cheap guesthouse at around $10 per night. Though unsettlingly reminiscent of Leonardo DiCaprio's guesthouse in *The Beach* (you know, the one where a murder takes place) I do a quick bed bug check, find none, and decide I like the price and reserve the room for the night.

I come to realize I have no idea what people do in Bangkok and, since I left my Southeast Asia guide book in the car back in the states on my way to the airport, genius that I am, I'm not going to get any closer to finding answers until I go outside.

Resolving not to let my solo-ness get to me, I walk around Khao San Road aimlessly for a few hours hoping to find some friendly tourists in the same boat.

It's hot and humid outside in a way that I haven't felt since Taipei. The air is so heavy and sweet, walking through it is like swimming in a sea of hot exhaust fumes as the motorbikes and taxis drive past, mixed with the aromas of street food.

There are chairs set up all along the street that seem to be dedicated to one of two things: massages or drinking beer. The difference is obvious since the beer-drinking chairs are plastic while the massage ones are canvas with foot rests in front. People peddle T-shirts and tank tops with the Rolling Stones or Rihanna on them or harem pants, which I lovingly refer to as hippie pants.

Street vendors sell Pad Thai – flat, wiggly rice noodles fried on a hot plate with tamarind paste, fish sauce, palm sugar, egg, bean sprouts, and tofu, garnished with a slice of lime. There are little jars with ground up peanuts, chilies, and dried shrimp to throw on as well to taste. I order a plate for the equivalent of USD $1 and savor the hot noodles. It's my first Thai dish and I find it to be delicious!

I'm unsuccessful at meeting much of anyone as most people are either in a pair or clearly on their way somewhere, trying to escape the oppressive heat. I waffle between being OK with walking around alone and freaking out just a little. I elect to return to my guesthouse for a much-needed shower and resolve to try again in the evening, when people will be a little more liquored up and (hopefully) friendlier.

6pm Khao San Road: I surprise myself by walking up to a group of friendly-looking tourists at a Pad Thai vendor and ask how the food is. We get to talking and I say, "I'm traveling alone and need some friends, have any room in your group?" I'm happy to find that it works like a charm. Perhaps my jet lag has me in a state unlike my normally shy and awkward self, but I like this new person.

I spend the rest of the night wandering around my new surroundings. The street is a lot livelier and crowded at night, with more vendors selling little toys, fake IDs, and offering custom suits. Despite the occasional overly touchy ping-pong show hecklers, I feel overwhelmed with joy at being back in Asia. I hadn't realized how much I had missed it.

I finish the night with a Thai massage for 100 Baht (about USD $3), get invited by my new friends to tour the islands in the south, but decide I'm simply not done with Bangkok yet.

I return to my guesthouse to see full-on construction carried out in the men's bathroom, just down the hall from me. I stick in my earplugs and fall asleep almost immediately. I awake with a start around 4am, almost forgetting where I am. It scares me at first, but then I feel OK with it.

It feels right to be here. I have been waiting for so long to make it happen, and now here I am.

Day two, I'm ready for you.

3

September 28, 2012

Day 2

I woke up around 6:30am happy to have made it that far despite jet lag. I looked around my tiny room and sighed, happy to be back in Asia – it felt so comfortable, like coming back home.

I emerged from my room and paid for another day at this hostel. It doesn't break the budget and I didn't get murdered in my sleep. Those are really my only requirements.

I walked outside into the humidity, heavy with the scent of street food and last night's beer, with the intention of visiting the Grand Palace – a gold-plated and mosaicked palace not far from Khao San Road. Immediately a tuk-tuk driver approached me and started asking me questions. I gave him honest and, what I now realize were probably the worst possible answers:

Him: Look at you! Such pretty white skin! Where you from? How long you been here?

Me: Um, thank you? California. I just got here yesterday. (Stupid, stupid, stupid.)

Him: You vote for Obama?

Me: Uhh, yes I did. And I would again. But I won't be home

for the election. (I decide against explaining the electoral vote system and the fact that California will go Democrat with or without my vote.)

Him: You been Bangkok before?

Me: First time!

Him: I take you tourist office! Get free map! Then I take you around Bangkok. Only 5 Baht!

I told him I needed some breakfast and sought refuge in a 7-Eleven. There are so many on Khao San Road that when standing in the doorway of one 7-Eleven, you can see another one just down the street. People do everything from paying bills and buying SIM cards to purchasing drinks and snacks there.

I emerged and, sure enough, he was waiting for me. I decided that, of all the tuk-tuk drivers, he put in the work and deserved my patronage. I told him change of plans: I wanted to go to the Royal Palace, but I still only wanted to pay 5 baht. I needed to change out of my short-shorts and sandals and I'd be right back.

I should have known that his insistence that shorts and sandals would be OK at the palace was a red flag. But I'm an eternal optimist to a fault.

And also maybe a little naive.

I hopped in the tuk-tuk and he powered on the motorbike it was attached to. Thai tuk-tuks are little canvas-covered wagons big enough for two people and they're easy to catch all over town.

We headed in what I didn't realize was the completely wrong direction. He dropped me at a tourist-booking agent and told me to go in and get a free map. Inside, I was told that the map costs 100 baht. I emerged a little confused and said I wanted to go to the palace. He acted annoyed that I hadn't booked any tours to the islands.

He then told me the palace doesn't open until 11am because of a Buddhist ceremony, but he'd be glad to take me to a bunch of other random sites around the city.

I told him to let me the heck out of his tuk-tuk because I'm well aware of this trick.

I climbed out with no idea where I was. My grand plans of getting to the palace early to avoid the crowds had been foiled. I broke down and bought a map at 7-Eleven, also for 100 baht (dangit!) and started wandering aimlessly – something I've come to perfect in the past couple of days!

A couple of other tuk-tuk drivers approached me, either selling me the same lie or quoting outrageous prices.

I cursed the universe of tuk-tuk drivers in Bangkok and decided they're all evil as I climbed into an air-conditioned cab with a driver who was willing to run his meter.

I finally arrived at the Palace and it was positively swarming with tourists – mostly Chinese speaking visitors, which I found kind of exciting because I got to practice my Mandarin when I asked them to take pictures of me (which they always praise after only a word or two).

I reached into my bag and took out my DSLR, found the perfect setting, the perfect angle, and the perfect statue, only to realize I hadn't put my SD card back in after loading pictures last week.

Cursing my dumbass series of moves, I whipped out my iPhone and started taking pictures, glad to have at least brought that along.

The palace looked like someone had taken a bunch of gold leaf and threw it around, all over statues of various guards and stupas. Gold tiling covered just about every wall and it was all quite intricate and enormous. In the heat of the day with the massive crowd of visitors, I couldn't handle a super long visit and elected to head back to my room after about thirty minutes.

I walked back to my guesthouse – yes, the palace was within walking distance all along – and saw the same tuk-tuk driver, who called out to me and asked if I had made it to the palace.

I nodded my head at him and said, "Yeah, it happens to open at 8:30! No Buddhist ceremonies today!"

He smiled and laughed an evil laugh. Instead of getting angry I just walked away. I knew thanks to my prior research that I'd encounter some frustrating things in Southeast Asia and this was the first test of my patience.

I'm not sure that I'd return to the Grand Palace, which feels like a tourist trap given the relatively high cost at USD $12 and truly insane crowds. Perhaps if I had actually arrived at 8:30am as planned, I would be singing a different tune.

That said, as I sit here in my room now I can appreciate that I learned a little something today. I'll have a little something to laugh about later, and hey, for only my second day in Bangkok, I think I've done alright.

Time to buy myself a celebratory Chang beer.

4

October 2, 2012

Day 5

After an initial stumble, Bangkok treated me well.

I ate, I drank (lots of mandarin orange juice and coconut slushies), and I was merry.

I bought hippie pants, and I soaked up the beginnings of what will be a long love affair between Southeast Asia and me.

I know it's early to call it, but I'm really digging it here.

Though today really tested the limits of my loving abilities.

I decided that it was time to leave Thailand after realizing that I didn't want to head up to Chiang Mai until the Lantern Festival (it takes place in November and it's presently only October), and didn't want to head down to the islands because, avid diver that I am, I want to wait for better conditions as it's still monsoon season and visibility is poor.

The next logical destination seems to be Siem Reap, Cambodia, to see the temple complex, Angkor Wat.

My morning began with haggling with taxi drivers to get a decent rate to the train station. At 5 AM on Khao San Road, not-a-one was willing to run the meter. After getting yelled at by ladyboys that 200 and 150 baht were good prices (who asked them, anyways?), I finally negotiated 100 baht and made my way to the station, where I paid half that for my 5-hour train ride to Aranyaprathet. From there I would take a tuk-tuk to Poipet, a seedy Cambodian border town, and eventually end up in Siem Reap, where I am now.

It all seemed so simple.

'Seemed' being the operative word.

The train itself was not badly priced at all. At only 48 baht (USD $1.50), for the third class train (the only option), I felt pretty good about my budget maintenance. I was in a roomy third class coach with open windows and fans that oscillated on the ceiling. It wasn't crowded at all and I was able to get my own row of seats all to myself. The view outside as we passed by little towns and rice paddies was lovely, and I smiled at the sunshine and the birds flying by.

Things started to get seedier after arriving in Aranyaprathet, where the tuk-tuk driver immediately took us to a fake "Cambodian Consulate" where they charge visitors an extra processing fee that is usually double the price. This border is rife with scams, and this is just one of many. They get away with it by masquerading as a visa service agency, which is legal, while passing some profit onto the tuk-tuk drivers who take unwitting tourists there. I had read up on this on the message boards the prior evening and knew better, and therefore walked to the actual border a few meters away.

At the real border crossing, once again they tried to scam me by asking for USD $25 rather than the posted $20 fee. I shook my head, pointed to the sign, and kept pushing my passport forward. Finally, after a group of Singaporean tourists overpaid and left the room, they obliged and I was on my way.

After getting into Poipet, the gross Cambodian border town littered with trash and loud, aggressive touts, I negotiated a shared $10 van after someone tried to sell me on a $60 taxi for the 2-hour ride out to Siem Reap. They tried to cheat me on my change, only giving me $4 back for my $20 bill, so I called them on it and got my correct money without much of a fight.

Honestly, why does everyone want to scam me?

After the 2-hour drive to Siem Reap, the driver took us to yet another set of tuk-tuk drivers, whom I've come to despise after my issue in Bangkok. They were meant to take us to our individual guesthouses.

Guesthouses, by the way, are typically small and affordable hotels and hostels with a combination of dorms and private rooms. They're quite common in Southeast Asia, and most backpackers and budget travelers stay in them.

Everyone else took off with no problem. My driver, of course, tried to get me to agree to either tip him $2 or hire him to take me to Angkor for $15 the next day. I just kept telling him "I don't know" and urged him to hit the road. He finally relented, took me to my hostel, and then put the full-court press on me again.

I shook my head "no" and went on my way. He then proceeded to curse me, my family, and everyone I've ever cared for or maybe just had pleasant thoughts about. The girls behind the front desk looked at me wide-eyed.

"What did you do to him?" they asked incredulously.

"I don't think I did anything," I replied, dejected.

I have been up since 5 AM. It is now 5 PM. I finally ate

something after barely eating all day and thinking it was time to accept that it's a failed day and I might as well call it a night.

Then, I headed to my shared room, immediately made three new friends, and felt better about the whole situation.

All in all, it only cost me $34, including my visa, to get from Bangkok to Cambodia. It wasn't the easiest method, but I made it in one piece, and it didn't break the bank.

Perhaps it was even a little adventurous, and one day, I'll look back on it fondly (but not right now).

Part 2

Cambodia: The True Land of Smiles

5

October 3, 2012

Day 6

I came to Cambodia with one goal in mind – I wanted to see Angkor Wat, which is the biggest religious monument in the world, covering over 162 hectares. It was originally constructed as a Hindu temple and eventually converted to a Buddhist temple which contributes to the amazing look of the architecture. The complex was built in the early 12th century and used to be the capital of the Khmer Empire, which means it is the ancient capital of Cambodia.

It is constructed in a series of galleries with pictures carved into sandstone rocks ranging from deities to animals and faces. The style is gentle and poetic as if the artists were moved by a divine power.

A moat runs along the galleries and walls of the main temple – Angkor Wat itself – and the other temples stretch on for miles, each with its own theme and claim to fame.

The ruins are overrun with vines and tree roots, making me feel like Indiana Jones as I walked through. The designs are harmonious, creating a feeling of peace within the stone galleries.

After my harrowing day of travel between Bangkok and

Siem Reap, I walked into my dorm to find a group of people who would become my friends and travel companions for the next few days. They're from different corners of the world – Australia, England, and New Zealand. We casually talked about our plans and elected to go to the temples at sunset together – something we've heard is quite beautiful and rumored to be even better than the famed sunrise.

To get to Angkor Wat, most people hire a tuk-tuk (usually to the tune of $15, a truly insane price in Cambodia where a dorm room only costs $2-$5 per night).

Instead, we decided to form an epic bike gang and pedaled out to Angkor Wat, happier with the $2 price tag for a bike rental.

Like a gaggle of geese we flew down the road, narrowly avoiding tuk-tuks, cars, motorbikes, and tourist vans, laughing all the way and enjoying the wind on our faces on the extremely hot and humid day.

I'm continuously blown away by everything I see in Cambodia and today was no different. On one side of me, a motorbike drove by with two adults and three children packed on, all of whom smiled and waved. On the other, the lovely moat around Angkor Wat and the intensely green jungle greeted me. Just ahead, an elephant crossed the road and a monkey scrambled by after him.

I kept pinching myself; it seemed like a dream. Every now and then I just paused, touched the sandstone and said to myself, "I'm in Cambodia right now. I'm really, truly in CAMBODIA right now."

Sometimes it's hard to grasp that it's all really happening and that I'm walking amongst this massive relic of history and devotion, this wonder of the world, after wanting to see it for as long as I can remember.

We rode right up to Angkor Thom, famous for giant faces carved into the sandstone, and climbed around for a while. A Cambodian guard congratulated us on coming in the afternoon after the tour busses and massive crowds had already left. I was amazed that tourists could walk right up and touch the ancient carvings. I imagined how it was back when it was a bustling capital hundreds of years ago, amazed it's somehow still standing after all that time, all of the wars, and the dark past.

The sun started to set, and we biked to what everyone calls the Tomb Raider temple: Ta Prohm. This one is famous for giant tree roots growing in and around the sandstone galleries. We were told it was closed for the evening, but we elected to go around to the other side and sneak in anyways. I'm sorry, it probably wasn't the right thing to do, but it ended up being the best move yet, as we had the temple almost completely to ourselves as the sun set.

We watched in awe as the sun dipped below the tree line – a red orb in the sky leaving trails of intense oranges and pinks behind in the clouds.

In that moment I didn't want to be anywhere else. Nothing else was on my mind. I'm still smiling from ear to ear and so happy with my present state of affairs as I write this. I can't imagine greener pastures anywhere else.

This, for me, is the best high in the world.

As the sky turned dark we hopped back on our bikes, all of which had lights powered by our pedaling.

The ride back proved to be a little scary in the dark as the roads were getting pretty crazy at that point, full of cars, tuk-tuks, and motorbikes. Luckily we made it back in one piece to start what was sure to be an amazing night of dancing in the street and ending at an all-Cambodian nightclub.

But that's a story for another time.

6

October 4, 2012

Day 7

After a long day spent playing around at Angkor Wat, the clock struck midnight and it was time to see what Siem Reap had to offer by way of nightlife. We deserved a round of Angkor beer after biking all around the temples, right?

Right.

Two dueling bars directly across the street from each other constitute the main nightlife for foreigners in Siem Reap on a street known as Pub Street.

You know you're at the right place if you look up and see a brightly glowing sign that proudly proclaims that the area is, indeed, "Pub Street."

At draft beer running about $1, the place gets more and more rowdy as the night goes on. We rolled up in a giant group from our hostel, doubling the crowd at pubs.

Our crew was awesome. We had a pair of Irish girls who took down grenades like they were water (a shot of tequila, Jäger, followed by Red Bull – I cannot drink these without ralphing, seriously), lazy-eyed Michael, a Melbourne-native who had the unlucky fortune of an eye infection at the time, Gemma, a super rad (I taught her the word "rad") chick from

London, and the ringleaders: a guy from England and a dude from Australia who had joined forces in Saigon and made their way to Siem Reap together. Their dynamic was hilarious and each raised the bar ever higher throughout the day with their humor. It was a good time.

With songs like "Gangnam Style" on loop, almost everyone at some point moved to the street between the two bars to join the parties together.

Then the sky opened up and rain started soaking everyone, most of whom couldn't have cared less and continued dancing to the music in the rain.

After we had our fun at Pub Street, we headed to an all-Cambodian nightclub known as Hip Hop. In contrast to Pub Street, which was full of foreigners, we were the only non-Cambodians at Hip Hop.

The locals all danced with us as we enjoyed the electro-style music and flashing pink and blue lasers. I felt welcomed and danced into the wee hours of the morning.

7

October 11, 2012

Day 14

I have found the ultimate oceanic sanctuary in Southeast Asia: Otres Beach in Southern Cambodia.

I know these are bold words, but from a girl who grew up with the beaches of Southern California and has traveled to many around the world since then, I'd have to say Otres Beach in Cambodia rivals Caye Caulker in Belize as one of the top offbeat beach destinations in the world, that I'm aware of, as it were.

I came here via Phnom Penh after the hostel owner at the place I stayed at in Siem Reap suggested this coastal town as the perfect spot to chill out. He was so right, and I'm thankful for the recommendation.

A lot of backpackers in Cambodia head down to Serendipity Beach in Sihanoukville – a beachside paradise with white sandy beaches and endless parties. Maybe it used to be a great place, but I saw it more as a cesspool of underage prostitution and tourist robberies.

Otres is just a few miles away and is known more as a hippie enclave (I mean, I have the pants now, so I'm in, right?). My guesthouse is a bunch of planks of untreated wood nailed together over an open-air bar and lounge area. The rooms are small, containing nothing but a mattress on the ground covered by a mosquito net, locked with a padlock and key. The water in the shared showers is room temperature, which is fine given the heat outside. Little geckos scurry all over the walls and ceilings chasing mosquitoes. I'm thankful they're there because the plentiful mosquitoes love me and it's unrequited.

Here is how a typical day goes:

As I'm lying on the white sand, so rich with silica that it squeaks beneath my feet, an elderly local Khmer woman comes by and gives me a full pedicure for just a few dollars. She also offers massage and threading services. Jack of all trades, this enterprising lady is.

Girls carrying baskets of fruit on their heads follow her closely; they offer fresh mango, pineapple, and small, sweet bananas. All of them wear hats made of straw that come to a point at the top and fan out in a circle, covering their faces from the sun. More likely to smear whitening cream on their beautiful copper-hued skin than to embrace it and let the sun kiss it, they cover up with long sleeves and pants, as well, something I can only imagine must be brutally hot in the 90+ degree weather with 90% humidity.

Restaurants along the beach sell whole, barbecued red snapper fish with rice and coleslaw for only $6 and I learn that I love the flavor of a fish with the bones still inside. The skin and especially the cheek of the fish are full of flavor and parts of it that I haven't had an opportunity to eat much back at home in California where it's typically just a fillet on the plate.

Though there are still children selling bracelets here, there are far fewer than in Sihanoukville where I was constantly heckled by either child vendors or Westerners trying to pass out flyers to get me in the bar they were working at.

I don't know about you, but that's not for me. I much prefer the sound of the white sands that squeak beneath my feet than techno beats. The water is like bath water. It's so clear I can see right through it to the bottom. There isn't any seaweed or sea grass floating through it and no waves to disrupt the calm sea, either. It's my first time in the Indian Ocean and it's a stark contrast to the sapphire-blue hue of the Pacific in California which is cold, full of seaweed, and has strong undertow thanks to the huge waves. Here in Cambodia, all is calm and clear.

Each night, especially those when the power goes off, I wade out into the calm, waveless sea and blue phytoplankton follows me like glitter falling out of my fingertips. It clings to my hair like pixie dust. I've never seen this kind of shimmering magic before, and I can't help but feel like they're just mirroring the sky full of stars. I'm shrouded in glittering beauty from my eyes to my toes, not worried about what might be in the water because I know from the daytime that nothing at all is in there to be scared of.

I fall into bed and sleep until the sun comes up again, bringing a heat with it that will draw me back into the perfect sea once more.

8

October 17, 2012

Day 20

Several days have passed, and I have no intention of leaving Otres anytime soon. Each day I wake up, push the mosquito net aside, and can't come up with a reason to leave. I'm in good company. Many of us travelers have been here for a while. I like that I tend to see the same friendly and familiar faces.

The only place in the area with Wi-Fi happens to be a bar called Richie's where patrons alternate between drafts of Angkor beer and dips in the pristine and calm sea.

A long-term patron of the bar announced to all of us today that we're a bunch of "misfits, losers, rejects! You couldn't survive a day in the real world!"

I looked at my phone and realized it was 1 PM on a Monday and almost everyone had a beer in his or her hand. I didn't feel one bit guilty. Being a misfit suits me just fine.

I hope this beach doesn't change; I know it's inevitable, and it will be rapid. But for now, with nothing but a dirt track that runs through the tiny town with cows roaming and grazing freely and a beach just a few steps away, I'm happy with this paradise.

9
—

October 24, 2012

Day 27

I arrived in Kratie, Cambodia last night after a nine-hour bus ride from Phnom Penh, a brief stopover after my two weeks along the Cambodian coast. The past few days have been a whirlwind of long journeys and I'm so tired of moving this quickly. I only came to Kratie on a whim, once again through word of mouth. It's famous for flat-nosed dolphins and it's my first time meeting the mighty Mekong River which I've often read about in books and seen in movies and was excited to finally see for myself.

A fellow guesthouse patron and I decided to hire bicycles today and ride around the Mekong through Kratie and to the smaller towns along the river. I really enjoyed the last time I rode bikes in Cambodia at Angkor Wat, so I had a feeling this would work out well, too.

We started down the road to the ferry and immediately the town faded away and a dirt road replaced it, surrounded by jungle-like flora, cows, free-roaming chickens and pigs, and one-room residences on stilts.

Kids ran out of the wooden shacks and yelled "hello!" in the cheeriest, brightest fashion.

They didn't just say it once either, they kept yelling it and waving enthusiastically. I felt the need to respond to each and every one. Sometimes practically singing "hellooo!" when a big group of them rode by.

I felt a little bit like a celebrity on the smallest scale possible. There I was, riding a rickety little bike with a tilting seat, wearing a Chang beer tank top (Khao San Road's finest), sweating like a pig, and yet I was the entertainment of the day.

Kiddies, I'm sorry. I didn't know I'd have an audience. I should have put on my Sunday best.

My Kratie companion, Jason, is a 30-year-old guy from Melbourne who took a short career break/dental vacation to Bangkok. It's common practice for Aussies to handle out-of-pocket dental and elective surgery procedures in Thailand, thanks to the much smaller price tag and competitive level of service.

He has a girlfriend back home and I'm happy that we're able to just hang out as nothing other than friends. He's a great companion and I enjoy his platonic company. He enjoyed saying hi to the children, too.

It was really nice to see them just enjoying life and going to school, donning freshly pressed uniforms with white shirts and blue shorts. So far in Cambodia, I've seen tons of children peddling bracelets or books on the street and in Angkor Wat. It's a tough thing to see children as young as 5 years old working.

Today, however, these kids appeared to just be kids. They weren't asking for money or candy, and they weren't trying to sell me anything. They just wanted to be acknowledged.

We ended up on some pretty remote little roads several

miles outside of Kratie, loving the sweeping grasses of the countryside and completely oblivious to the fact that we were headed farther and farther into the middle of nowhere.

Jason shouted to me, "By the way, I'm not the best with directions!"

To which I responded, "Perfect! I have no sense of direction at all!"

We passed a few waving men but figured they were simply saying hello as well, so we casually waved back and kept going. Eventually, as the rain started to come down softly, we decided to stop when yet another adult waved.

We learned a valuable lesson that day: when a kid in Kratie yells out to you, wave. When an adult yells out to you, stop and find out what the heck you're doing wrong.

He pointed us in the right direction and we were on our way back to the river, where we were meant to be all along.

I mean, really, you'd think a giant river like the Mekong would be hard to lose.

A couple of times, my pesky bike seat tilted so much that I needed a helping hand. Luckily, both times I stopped at a random shack that appeared to hold promise of a possible wrench, an eager and friendly local helped me and expected nothing in return. Both times, I was surrounded by kids saying hello over and over.

The rain never let up but it was welcome as it was more of a light sprinkling than a downpour. It provided relief on an otherwise sweltering hot day.

We spent the better part of the day biking around the Mekong River, followed by a subdued evening with a couple of other travelers in a very quiet Kratie (the king has died and Cambodia is finishing up a week of silence in his honor). We went to the night market and ate some BBQ with Khmer spices on it.

Apart from the unique and savory spice rub on Khmer BBQ, Cambodia doesn't have a lot of its own ethnic food, save for luk-lak, which is pieces of fried beef served with a limey and tangy Kampot peppercorn sauce, and amok curry which is a fish curry served in banana leaves.

As I write this I realize and fully accept that tomorrow will probably involve sore muscles and loads of tingly menthol camphor Tiger Balm, but I'll worry about that then. Today, I'm still in the afterglow of a beautiful day in the countryside – something I've been craving ever since I arrived in Cambodia.

10

October 27, 2012

Day 30

Day by day I fall more intensely in love with Cambodia. Each place I encounter is more beautiful and impressive than the last, and that's saying a lot considering I started with Siem Reap – home to Angkor Wat.

Some people say that Thailand is the land of smiles, but I suspect they haven't been to Cambodia.

Considering the hardship and genocide these people went through so recently, so many of them experiencing it firsthand, it's so humbling to see the way they love life, even with so little by way of possessions and money.

It's like each day here provides a new lesson to be learned about the beauty of life and how to appreciate it.

I haven't had a hot shower in weeks – I don't even remember what they feel like anymore. Nowadays, the cold water is welcome after a hot day covered in a glaze of DEET and humidity.

I've done nothing but share rooms, usually full of bunk beds, for nearly the full month I've been traveling. My bed often consists of a slightly sandy and damp mattress with a mosquito net covering – usually a holey one. If I encounter soap in a bathroom I'm completely astounded and delighted. I can't remember what air conditioning feels like. Sometimes I don't even have a fan or electricity for most of the day. I spent a good chunk of this month in a damp existence covered in sweat, seawater, or some mixture of the two.

The best part is I couldn't care less. I've gladly traded all of the comforts of Western life for this Cambodian lifestyle and I don't miss them at all. I look at my makeup bag and laugh now. There's no way that's going on my face.

I'm kind of shocked at how little I really need to be happy. Is this what traveling does to people? I think so.

Every day here is like a new intense high. I wake up and pinch myself, completely understanding how some travelers come here planning on a few weeks and end up staying for months, or even years.

I'll wear this place like a thumbprint on my heart forever. It has changed me for the better.

Part 3

Laos: The Land of Mighty Water

11

October 30, 2012

Day 33

It was around 4:30 in the afternoon and it hit me as I was floating down the Mekong River in 4000 Islands, Laos, that this is bliss. There was a group of backpackers behind me, occasionally sticking their arms in the water to swim against the current and laughing as we struggled to remain one big mass of inner tubes, hand in hand, passing a bottle of Beer Lao around.

A dazzling double rainbow lit up the sky before me. Unobstructed, we could see the entirety of the two arcs in their full glory, appearing as a gateway back to Don Det, the one island out of the 4,000 I'm staying on.

We had just come from a beach BBQ on a tiny island where local monks plant and harvest vegetables. When they're not around, two tiny kittens guard it. They happily shared their space with us today in exchange for a few bites of fresh river fish and a scratch behind the ears.

It's a Tuesday and I can't help but think back to what I was doing a year ago today, slumped in my cubicle and wishing for days like this.

4000 Islands sits just north of the border in Cambodia. A

bus ride then a quick boat jaunt from the mainland gets you to the hippie haven of Don Det, which attracts a chill crowd of travelers who spend most of our time lazily reading books and swapping travel stories on decks over the Mekong River. At the moment it's brown from the rainy season, but I'm told it's a lovely and clear green during the drier months.

The otherwise rural stretch of islands is dotted with modest bungalows on stilts that cater to the backpacker crowd. They range anywhere from $3-$6, depending on whether they have an attached bathroom or not. One can easily stay a week here without needing to spend much money at all. I splurged and took a $6 bungalow, which I sometimes feel guilty for but love having my own space, even if only for a short while. It doesn't have much other than a bamboo chair, pink mosquito net, and a double bed, plus an attached bathroom with a push toilet (flushed by throwing buckets of water into the bowl), and a cold-water shower.

Some people complain that there's not much to do here on Don Det, but they simply haven't looked around. Kayaking tours take off daily in the early morning for the sporty travelers who feel like baking in the sun and getting an epic arm workout (read: not me).

But I did cycle around Don Det and crossed the bridge to neighboring Don Khong Island to view the waterfalls and the sandy beach.

The roads, as I'm seeing often in Southeast Asia, are packed dirt filled with potholes, which only adds to the fun and sore bum thereafter.

Yes, 4000 Islands is the life. The sun set created a dazzling hot pink display, and we lost count as we tried to see if there really are, indeed, 4000 tiny islands. We pulled up to the shore of Don Det as some locals called out "sai ba dee" (hello) to us.

I'm writing to you as I bask in the evening warmth, my skin tanned to a deep yellow-brown thanks to the sun today and my hair wet from the shower. It's nearly dinnertime, but I simply had to update you while it was still fresh in my mind.

Tonight, we'll probably do what we do every night: lie around and talk about how we spent our Tuesday, trying to connect to the weak Wi-Fi to upload our Instagram photos, pressing 'retry' a few times, and finally giving up to accept the present moment. It's the right thing to do, anyways.

After all, who needs the interwebs when you have the river below your feet, good company all around, and another day of laziness (or biking, tubing, kayaking, etc.) ahead of you? Not this girl, certainly not this girl.

12

November 4-6, 2012

Days 38-40

When I embarked on this solo journey I promised myself I'd seek off-the-beaten-path adventures and take myself out of my comfort zone. I knew that becoming comfortable on a motorbike was one of the biggest challenges I would face. Five years earlier when I studied abroad in Taiwan, I had dubbed them "chariots of doom" and refused to get on one for the entire eight months I lived there after seeing an accident on my second night in Taipei. I had other options, such as public transit, taxis, and my feet.

In Southeast Asia, however, sometimes there is no other option to get where you want to go than to take a motorbike. The Bolaven Plateau, famous for amazing landscapes and waterfalls, is one of those places. I knew the day would come that I'd travel to a place I couldn't handle missing just because of the transport issue, and after a little over a month into my trip, sure enough, it had arrived.

Backpackers often skip the Bolaven Plateau in southern Laos in favor of the more popular northern destinations of Luang Prabang and Vang Vieng, which is famous for the river tubing. Yet I'd heard it's absolutely stunning and a chance to see a part of Laos that isn't populated with tourists yet. Since I was heading north from 4000 Islands and it was on the way, I figured it was time to confront my fears and give the Bolaven Plateau loop a try.

I arrived in Pakse the prior night. The city doesn't have much to offer to tourists, but that didn't stop my newfound friends and me from hanging out with a local guesthouse owner who later took us to an all-Lao nightclub until the wee hours of the morning. I found this new group when, upon walking into the cheapest guesthouse in town, which was more of a hotel than a guesthouse and a bit out of my budget, I called out to a girl sitting in the lobby, asking, "Is it nice here?"

She replied with an English accent that it was lovely and invited me to come sit with her after I checked in, which I did. Before I knew it we were out dancing at a Laotian nightclub, clanking glasses with locals and laughing under purple and pink laser lights. It was a flashback to my good times in Siem Reap with locals sharing their beer with me and jiving to the bumping music. I could have stayed behind in Pakse longer, drawn in by the nightclub night after night, but I had a plan that involved a motorbike and some waterfalls, after all.

The next morning, my heart pounding, I met up with Magnus, a Danish guy with quotes to just about every recent American comedy memorized, a head of curly blonde hair and a genuine, honest smile. Together with a few others we rented three motorbikes for six bikers from our guesthouse. Score! I wasn't going to have to drive! However, I was going to have to put my life in Magnus' hands.

I initially met him on the islands in Cambodia, ran into him again at Otres Beach, and yet again in 4000 Islands. When we saw each other there, we agreed to meet up a few days later in Pakse to drive the loop. I'd known him for a few weeks, which was longer than anyone else, so I concluded that it was enough to give him the reins. The friends he brought along were two German girls and a newly married young German couple. They were all incredibly sweet and happy to practice their English with me.

Luckily the roads are somehow mostly paved in and around the Bolaven Plateau, unlike every other road in Laos, and despite the occasional pig, cow, goat, dog, or chicken running into the road, they are more or less traversable without issue.

The main reason why people motorbike out to this region is to check out the beautiful waterfalls. Typically, tourists take the afternoon to head to one large and famous waterfall and then head back to Pakse.

But we were ever the ambitious travelers and decided to do the full 4-day loop, but in just 3 days.

The highlights for me included the happy children who waved hello (which reminded me of the enthusiastic kids in Kratie, Cambodia), the locals in the back of a truck who handed us bananas as we drove by (it was a hilarious exchange – props to Magnus for engineering it by getting just close enough to the truck without crashing), and of course, feeling the mist on my face at my favorite waterfall, Tad Gneuang.

It was a huge waterfall, like they all were, really, that seemed to have come straight out of a fantasy movie. The rainforest all around it was gorgeous, full of huge trees, swinging vines, monkeys playing in the distance, and lots of pretty white flowers growing out of the grasses in the mist.

I was in complete awe of the scenery in Laos. I'd thought Cambodia was beautiful, but honestly, Laos' scenery blows it away. I kept singing "Welcome to the Jungle" by Guns N' Roses to myself in my head whilst taking in all of the different plants, giant butterflies, and ample waterfalls. Each one seemed more spectacular and remote than the last.

We saw a total of five waterfalls during our trip, and, can you imagine, we didn't even see all that there were to see!

Today was our final day, in the remote outskirts of Sekong where nobody speaks English and I never saw another Westerner, I silently thanked the powers that be, whatever they may be, for letting me experience such a lovely place. Then we blasted back off to Pakse, me trying not to think about the possibility of crashing into a pig and Magnus trying to sneak up another 10k or so on the speedometer when he thought I wasn't paying attention.

Somehow I've managed to meet so many more amazing people than I'd ever imagined. Each day seems better than the last.

I keep turning over something in my mind that a fellow traveler with years of experience under her belt told me a month prior: "Enjoy the beginning, because nothing will ever be this amazing and wonderful ever again."

Is she jaded? How could anything be better than traveling the world, constantly meeting new people and seeing a new horizon every day if I so chose?

What happened to her that made her stop loving this? Maybe one day I'll find out but for now, I can't fathom it.

13

November 7-10

Days 41-44

Vientiane is the capital of Laos and the next stop on my journey as I move north through the country. The former French colonialism is evident here in the architecture, and while there isn't much sightseeing to do, it's charming, and I can't help but like this town.

I was sitting across from Blake, the black-haired and big-brown-eyed hostel manager at Vientiane Backpacker's Hostel where I had planned to spend only one night to take care of a Thai tourist visa. I had just connected to the horrendous Wi-Fi and had enough time, between loading pages and trying in vain to write a few blog posts, to get to know him as a Texan who had come to Laos on a whim and picked up a job at the hostel.

Feeling a little more blunt than usual, I quipped, "Why in the world would travelers take jobs at hostels in exchange for room and board when the compensation works out to be, like, $2 hourly? That just seems ridiculous."

He pointed to an impressive mural on the wall of a giant tree with an imaginative planetary system around it and swirling lines and curves within the trunk, reminiscent of a maze, and said they had made that very offer to the artist. I replied, "Well that's arts and crafts time! That's a completely different deal than serving drinks and handing out party flyers."

"Then why don't you do it?" He prodded, slyly.

As easily as that, we hatched a plan. I was going to paint an elephant mural, the hostel mascot, on a free hostel wall in the lobby in exchange for room and board, and beer, of course.

I was about to paint the largest piece I had ever attempted by far, mixing all of my own colors and creating the work completely freehand. Additionally, I hadn't painted for nearly five years, and all I had done were impressionistic landscapes before, but I didn't really advertise that last bit of information.

They were blindly putting their faith in me.

Crazy Michael, the hunchbacked Vietnamese hostel owner with exactly one speaking volume, which is one decibel above shouting, had me jump on the back of his motorbike and with that, we were off to the paint store – an overstuffed Home Depot-like retailer all squashed into a few square feet of space. All kinds of tools and wares were stuffed onto the shelves. It was almost cartoonish, and I couldn't imagine how anyone working there could possibly know where everything was located. Still, he found the paint and brushes without much searching and we bought red, blue, and yellow paint, two brushes, and some paint thinner.

I wasn't exactly sure what to create and elected to take a walk around the Buddhist temple across the street while I searched for inspiration. A young monk in a bright orange robe saw me walking around and smiled a huge smile full of straight white teeth and said, "Sai ba dee!"

A moment later a light bulb went on in my head and a tattooed elephant came to mind, wearing all of the symbols of life I saw on the temple walls. The repeating flower and vine patterns coated in gold that snaked and curled around the walls of the temple were so beautiful they seemed the perfect colorful covering for an elephant that was as tall as I was. It was going to be a big project.

Day one was spent sketching, nervously looking to Michael and Blake for approval, and trying to ignore the pressure of onlookers. I hadn't considered that I'd have an audience throughout the entire process.

Today I got to work finishing the painting, listening to music, and sweating in the blistering Vientiane heat.

Every now and then someone stopped by and looked pensively at my work then gave me a thumbs up. This helped me tremendously because, to be honest, sometimes I'm insecure and I need approval, especially when attempting a style of art that I've never tried before.

The final product turned out better than I expected. The elephant is covered in green vines and orange flowers turning to yellow as they move across his body plus purple and yellow tapestries mirroring the style of the flowers in the wat across the way. I put my heart and soul into it, and it shows.

I patted myself on the back, inadequately washed the paint off of my arms, and settled in across from the painting, taking it in and realizing I'd probably never see it with my own eyes again.

I leave Vientiane tomorrow – three days after I had originally planned. I suppose that's the serendipity of travel and I'm grateful to have left a little piece of myself behind here.

I take everything I said about working at a hostel back. I'll happily paint in exchange for room, board, and beer any time.

14

November 12, 2012

Day 46

It was a lazy afternoon near the Blue Lagoon in Laos, just up the road from the infamous river tubing in Vang Vieng. I made my way up to the little riverside town after painting a mural and finally reuniting with my Bolaven Plateau crew, including Magnus, happy to see them again.

I largely spent the day jumping from tree branches into the deeply aquamarine-blue lagoon and sitting on the swing that sat just an inch or so above the cool water. The heat of the day made it the perfect activity.

"It's the best thing," said a tall, green-eyed and dirty blonde-haired Australian next to me, "to climb through the cave, then come cool off in the lagoon. You've got to try it."

So far on the trip nobody had really caught my attention, but suddenly I was completely taken off guard, entranced. Who was this tall drink of water and where did he come from? I didn't notice him walk up but suddenly he was all I could see. Everything else faded away into a cloud of blue mist and it was just us right here on that swing, kicking our feet in the water playfully. He had a magnetism to him, and I was drawn in by the pull.

"Let's see what's in the cave!" my friends yelled, pulling me out of my trance abruptly.

Sure, I figured, best to walk away from this one and explore. It's not the right time to get distracted by a man. Not when there's a cave to tour. I said I'd catch him later, hoping it would be true, and made my way over to join my crew.

We climbed up the steep stairs to the cave entrance just as the clock struck 4:30. Surely it would be a quick jaunt, wouldn't it?

We made it several yards through what turned out to be quite a slippery and steep pathway, or lack thereof, around the rocks. Just as we started to descend into total darkness, the light of my headlamp waned and eventually fizzled. Magnus and I saw a light ahead and decided to leap and bound around the rocks separating us from what was surely another party descending the depths of the cave. Perhaps we could join them.

It was three other people all navigating the cave with nothing more than a dying iPhone light. Sure we could join! The more the merrier, they said.

We ventured deeper and deeper into the cave. It eventually became apparent that we were most likely spending more time in the cave than we had originally budgeted. Of course, I didn't have anything useful like a watch, so I had no idea of the time. Magnus had removed his prior to jumping into the lagoon. Oh well, we were already in it too deep, literally and figuratively.

We had no choice but to keep with the group that adopted us, as they were the only ones with a way to light our eventual exit.

The sun had already set by the time we finally ventured out just as the iPhone light died. We made our way down the steep steps to reunite with our friends at the bottom of the hill. They were the only ones left at the lagoon, and they applauded our return. They'd worried we'd never come out.

There were no tuk-tuks left at that hour, so our choice was to pile three of us – all grown adults much larger than a typical Lao native – onto one motorbike and drive over the rocky road in the dark back to our bungalows.

Magnus took the reins; I was sandwiched in the middle, and our friend Felix barely clung onto the back.

"Felix?" Magnus muttered, "Are you clinging to my waist?"

I lost it and couldn't stop laughing for the rest of the ride.

To make matters even worse (or more hilarious), the horn was stuck and beeped intermittently for no apparent reason. I was laughing uncontrollably, out of fear, really, all while Magnus drove like the wind over rocks, sand, and gravel and Felix whimpered behind me. I knew Magnus was good on those roads. He'd been driving me around Laos like a champ all week in the Bolaven Plateau.

We made it the few miles to the bungalow in one slightly shaken piece. After the elation of surviving wore off, the Australian from the lagoon swing came right back into my mind.

I wonder if I'll see him again.

15

November 13, 2012

Day 47

It was late at night at the Irish bar in Vang Vieng after a day of tubing down the river with the Australian, who it turns out has a name – Joshua. We ran into each other last night after the motorbike fiasco, and he invited me for an adventure the following day. How could I say no?

Vang Vieng was once famous for a giant party that took place down the river in inner tubes. There were bars all along the banks serving up strong buckets and bad decisions. There were ziplines that people could jump on and ride into the river which was entirely too shallow and caused a lot of deaths as a result. After some pressure from the Australian government, all of the bars had to shut down. That was only a couple of months ago and now there are only a few people tubing down the river each day.

I clearly don't know how it used to be since I never experienced Vang Vieng in all of its hedonistic glory, but tubing down the river today was a beautiful and peaceful experience. It seems a raucous party would just ruin my favorite aspect of it – the nature.

The river runs through a jungle with giant rocks that seem

to show up out of nowhere, as if placed there by a giant. They aren't gradual and have no slopes; they just appear. It was a wonderland of green and purple as we tubed down, giant fireflies landing on my toes and little kids swimming up to the tubes, hitchhiking a swim.

After an afternoon in inner tubes in the sun, Joshua sat across from me and it was just the two of us. His friend had already gone to bed after starting the day a bit too early with a breakfast screwdriver and continuing the party all day.

Joshua is only on a three-week trip. I told him I'd just begun an indefinite journey. Emerald-green eyes sparkling, lips smirking, he said something to me that struck a chord.

"In my experience, long-term travelers are either running from something, towards something, or are genuinely just traveling to travel, but 99% of the time it's one of the first two."

Without much hesitation, I said, "I'm definitely running away," which I retracted only a moment later to say, "But, no, I just really like traveling. I've wanted to for as long as I can remember."

The smirk turned into a laugh. It's clear that not even I know what I'm really doing. I've insisted from the beginning that this is not some sort of *Eat, Pray, Love* "finding myself" endeavor in Southeast Asia. I already know myself, don't I?

So then what is all this really about?

I looked at the sea of backpackers filling the bar around me and wondered the same about them. Plenty of us have been on the road for a while, and we all speak of our displeasure at the thought of having to return home eventually. Traveling is like some parallel universe we all want to remain in forever, avoiding the "real" world of suits and ties and taking in all that we can, in all of the ways we can, with all of the people we can.

So what is it that we're running from? Obligations? Mortgages? The American (or English, or Australian, or German, or hell, Uruguayan) dream of settling down with a white picket fence, porch swing for two, 2.5 children, a dog named Fido and a cat named Fluffy?

Or if we're running towards something, is it a better understanding of ourselves, the world around us, or a set of photos we can point to one day and proudly say, "I went there, I did that!"?

When the travel does eventually end, as it will for all of us, what will we be left with? This question terrifies me every time I try to confront it.

So yes, I'm running. I have made no secret of my distaste of the previous four "grey" years spent in an equally grey cubicle with a maddening routine.

I'm definitely still looking for something. I don't know what, though. I wonder if I'll ever know or if I'll ever desire to stop searching.

The clock struck 11 and, given Laos has a curfew, the bars closed and everyone poured out onto the street. The next move for everyone was to sing songs in a circle while someone played guitar, or more commonly to head over to the bamboo bridge and test its ability to hold hundreds of people.

Joshua invited me to walk with him over the bamboo bridge to continue our conversation. Nothing happened between us that night other than some cuddling, but the attraction was undeniable.

It's terrifying, too, because I didn't foresee an encounter like this so early into my trip. I don't want anything to compromise this journey I'm on, but I can already see a storm coming from a mile away.

16

November 18, 2012

Day 52

Magnus left this morning from our shared bungalow before I returned. I neglected our friendship over the past few days and I feel bad, but my days have been filled with river water, sun, and of course, Joshua.

He and I have the same sense of humor. He's a writer, too, a musician, and incredibly well spoken. I keep asking the universe why he showed up now, fewer than two months into my trip that is supposed to be all about me. Little by little, I cautiously ask myself if it should be a little bit about him, too.

Our days are numbered, though. I'm following him to Luang Prabang, a place I planned to go anyways, but he's returning back to Melbourne after a brief stint in Vietnam and I'm staying here in Laos.

Luang Prabang is a fabulous little town. Like Vientiane, the French colonial past is evident here from the architecture and ubiquitous baguettes at breakfast cafes and sandwich stands. There's a night market that serves up all-you-can-pile-onto-your-plate noodles and veggies for just over a dollar, and within the market there are all kinds of neon orange and green Hmong wares. Joshua bought a painting to remember the trip by, and I bought a few more pairs of hippie pants because I can't get enough.

There are a few waterfalls outside of town that look like cascading pools of periwinkle water, much like the blue lagoon back in Vang Vieng but on steroids. It feels like it's all coming full circle. We met and we'll say goodbye in water that is a color I've never seen before now with a person I never imagined could exist in this world until now.

"Come with me to Mui Ne in Vietnam for a few days," he said to me this morning. I told him I can't. It's not in my finances. It's not in my plans. It's not the right thing for me to do right now.

They're just words with no meaning, and he knows that deep down, I'm dying to join him. It'll extend this fling by just a few days and then we'll say goodbye, and that's what keeps me from pulling the trigger. Why get more attached for no reason? It seems irresponsible of both of us.

He just left to buy his ticket as I sit in the room writing down my feelings.

Twenty minutes have passed, and now there's a curveball. Joshua just popped back in and announced, "I'll buy your ticket and your visa. It's not that expensive. I'll fly you to Thailand after so that you can attend the lantern festival just like you planned to. It won't mess with your plans too much."

We went back and forth a few times but he's very convincing. Why not just give it another few days, right? It could be a storybook romance or just another fling. There's only one way to know for sure.

17

November 23, 2012

Day 57

I flew out to Mui Ne a few days ago, and the feelings progressed between Joshua and me. We're learning more about each other with each passing day, and I like this person who came floating into my life.

He finds my obsession with passion fruit to be endearing and ensured that he shared his with me each morning we were together. He and his friend searched out a restaurant last night where we got the closest thing possible to a Thanksgiving dinner which was a grilled fish and some potatoes that arrived well after the meal, but it's the thought that counts.

There's just something about him that's special. Well, actually, there are a lot of things. His laugh is amazing, his gentle voice calms me, and I love the way he says certain words with that Aussie accent. I'm toast, I tell you.

We had a fantasy-like romance over the past ten days, and I've started to question my sanity. I'm unable to see anything but him in the future, and I feel like I'm losing grip of my trip of a lifetime.

Here's the kicker: Before he left, he asked if I would be his girlfriend. I didn't have to think very long about it. He seems perfect to me – smart, handsome, funny, and artistic. Despite a little voice in the back of my head that said, "It hasn't been long enough since you left your last relationship, you need more time," I said yes.

He understands that I need to finish my trip and we made plans for him to visit me over New Year's in the Thai Islands. It won't be that long apart. It'll work out somehow.

I know this seems ridiculous, but haven't crazier things happened? Can you really have it all? I guess I'll find out.

Part 4

Thailand: The Land of Conflicting Emotions

18

November 30, 2012

Day 64

Joshua's gone, and I spent an uneventful week in Chiang Mai catching up on these entries and eating good street food. I somehow managed to completely miss the lantern festival because the locals like to cut down on the amount of tourists at the event by claiming it's canceled and being cryptic about the location. It's a bummer because it's the only thing I actually planned out for this whole trip. *C'est la vie*, right?

Now I'm back in the traveler's grind, but suddenly something very big is missing: my heart and soul. It seems to have left with Joshua right back to Melbourne, and I feel a void. I've elected to try to fill it by heading to the one spot that everyone says is utter perfection: Pai. It's a two-hour winding bus ride away from Chiang Mai, and I'm ready for some nature now.

See you on the other side, hopefully in paradise.

19

December 1-7, 2012

Days 65 - 71

I've done pretty well at seeking out offbeat, hippie destinations in each of my countries so far. In Cambodia it was Otres Beach and in Laos it was Don Det, and, while quite different from each other, both provided a laid-back vibe in a beautiful locale. Pai really takes the cake, though. It takes the sweetest, most colorful, most eccentric cake imaginable.

In one day I run into Thailand's version of Captain Jack Sparrow – he sits under the bridge and never breaks character. He invites you to send him an email at captainjacksparrow@hotmail.com. I can't believe that email isn't already taken but I don't test it out, either. I also learn to spin fire poi at the circus school, take yoga classes, and run around a narrow yellow canyon and hang out in hammocks.

What I love about Pai is there is no standard mode of operation. Nobody cares how you dress or act and nobody really minds. Everyone wears hippie pants, a clear indication that these are my people, and pretty much everyone embraces each other and makes friends. The setting is rural and beautiful, and I feel completely free.

I'm staying in a place made out of bamboo and palm fronds

surrounded by rice paddies in various stages of growth. It's all open-air dorms of just basic mattresses and mosquito nets. I find the thing about mosquito nets is, no matter how basic the accommodation, they make every bed seem like a princess bed, shrouded in a lovely white netting that cascades around the sides of the mattresses.

Daily, I drive myself around the beautiful countryside on my motorbike through winding, steep roads, finally embracing the motorbike and realizing that the freedom it gives me is addictive.

I can't believe I refused to drive one of these for so long. There's really nothing to be scared of on roads that are this devoid of traffic. Almost all my fears are removed and I have fun driving through canyons that would have terrified me months earlier.

I learned when a few mornings ago my new friend Alex, a relaxed Uruguayan dude with light brown hair about my color and kind green eyes, offered to take me to the bike rental place. He pulled over less than halfway there, climbed off the bike and announced that I'd be driving us the rest of the way. I protested that I had no idea what I was doing and he replied, "This is how you learn. How are you going to truthfully tell them you have experience riding a motorbike otherwise?"

I couldn't believe he was willing to put his life, quite literally, in my hands. I reluctantly climbed on and slowly turned the right handlebar, the method for engaging the gas and making the bike move forward. It was surprisingly easy and actually quite fun!

Pai feels nothing like the rest of Thailand. It doesn't even necessarily feel like you're in Thailand at all when in Pai, but, if I'm honest, that doesn't bother me at all. It's a parallel universe and that makes it fabulous.

There are waterfalls to slide down with cute little Thai boys at the bottom who help you out of the pool of cool water. There are waterfalls to swim under and jump off of, and there are land cracks to stop for lunch in where the owner brings out a spread of hibiscus fruit juice, potatoes, tamarind, and most importantly, passion fruit. He doesn't charge a fee, and instead sets out a box for donations.

All in all, Pai is one of my favorite places I've visited so far on this trip. It is a vegan-friendly, designer tea, bamboo-tattooed, rainbow-haired (really, a friend of mine got a rainbow hair dye-job here), dreadlocked paradise in one of the most beautiful settings imaginable. I've made friends here I'll never forget and will always cherish. I made memories here I'll always hold dear.

Go to Pai. You'll be glad you did.

20

December 8, 2012

Day 72

After one week in Pai I finally tore myself away. I met a group of three other girls there whom I got along with immediately and we've formed a pretty strong bond. There's Freya from Scotland who has a very similar background to mine, Emma from England who is both direct and absolutely hilarious, and Kylie from Canada, the youngest and also a bundle of laughs. We're of varying ages but have a lot in common: We're all solo travelers, we all have brown hair and blue eyes, and we seem to have the same silly sense of humor. They're in Laos now and while they're over there I'm spending some time in Chiang Rai for another big highlight of Northern Thailand: the famous White Temple.

The White Temple has been on my bucket list ever since the first time I laid eyes on photos of it. It looked incredible, and also artsy and creepy, like the Buddhist counterpart of Barcelona's Sagrada Familia. The two have similarities – both were built in the modern era and neither has been completed yet.

The White Temple was started in 1997 and will remain

under construction until 2070. The Sagrada Familia is supposed to be finished in 2030.

My complete lack of planning got me into trouble again today as I attempted to visit the White Temple. Normally, one can easily catch a bus to the temple for only 20 baht (less than $1). Ever confident in my awful sense of direction I foolishly headed out without a map. I used the only one I had last night to fight the mosquito infiltration in my room and didn't want to carry a paper soaked in mine or someone else's potentially malaria-infested blood around with me.

I walked in the 90-degree heat for 30 minutes and realized I had no idea where I was going. I stepped into a 7-Eleven where a tiny woman took pity on me and offered to call me a taxi. "Bus station very far," she said. I replied that I feared the taxi was expensive, but she negotiated with him over the phone to use the meter so that it would cost about the same as the bus then brought me to what appeared to be a gynecologist's office to wait for the taxi.

The curious stares from pregnant Thai women probing me, I waited, and waited, and waited. The taxi finally showed up and tried not to use the meter. After some back-and-forth, I paid more than I wanted to and finally found myself at the temple. Luckily, entrance was free.

The entrance to the temple is framed by creepy white hands reaching out from the depths of hell holding skulls and occasionally flipping the bird. Some even have ruby-red fingernails. As one progresses down the walkway to two angels on either side, gilded in mirror patterns to reflect the glittering sun, the setting changes from hell to paradise. The patterns curl and swirl around creating one of the most unique and enchanting works of art and architecture I've ever seen.

Inside there's a rather curious mural with *Kung Fu Panda*, *Sailor Moon*, scenes from *The Matrix*, and other pop culture references. Apparently this temple is meant to speak out against the dangers of alcohol and cigarettes, but I just see it as one trippy wonderland – the manifestation of what must have been one crazy dream.

I scurried into the temple area, eagerly snapping pictures, prancing around trying to get every angle of the amazing hands.

There was a man with a loudspeaker who eventually noticed I was holding up the stream of people steadily piling through the narrow temple paths. "Lady, keep moving, keep moving!" he said as I chuckled and kept snapping pictures.

I looked through my photos and wasn't satisfied so I had to go through once again, and I hoped my friend with the microphone didn't notice. Then again, I was one of the only foreigners there, and I was wearing purple elephant hippie pants and a bright pink T-shirt. I'm not sure how or why I thought I'd scurry past him successfully. I started my photo snapping again.

Sure enough, he noticed me right away and got right back on his microphone: "Lady! Keep moving, keep moving!" I started giggling again as I slowly started to oblige.

Determined to take the bus back, I successfully found the bench under the tree on the highway to the right of the giant photo of the king and made my way home for 20 baht. Today was a good day all in all and resulted in some amazing photos and hilarious memories. It's the first day I've spent alone since

I arrived in Bangkok over two months ago, and for some reason it's okay with me. Perhaps that's because Joshua and I were chatting all day, and we'll Skype in a moment.

Actually, that's him ringing now.

21

December 9, 2012

Day 73

Sukhothai had big shoes to fill after my magical week in Pai and the impressiveness of the White Temple in Chiang Rai. I was feeling slightly blue for leaving that colorful town at all and a little sore after spending 6 hours on a bus to get to Sukhhothai.

I wasn't sure what I would think of this new place, the first capital of Thailand, but when I alighted from the bus, I was immediately warmly greeted by a driver from my guesthouse, a courtesy I hadn't been party to yet in Thailand. Things were immediately off to a good start given I didn't have to deal with my nemeses – tuk-tuk drivers.

This little pocket of Thailand is split into two towns: the old and new. Most guesthouses are located in the New Sukhothai – a small town full of friendly people and smiling faces.

I'd heard that the ruins of Sukhothai warranted a look and were even impressive enough to rival some of the ruins in the Angkor Wat complex. Like Pai, this town wasn't even on my radar before leaving home for this journey. I'm glad I stopped by as it was impressive, indeed.

I met a friendly German guy, Johannes, and a quirky

Canadian girl, Louise, on the rickety songthaew (a pickup truck with bench seats in the back) ride over from the new town. We rented bicycles for $1 and made our way to the first set of ruins, Wat Mahathat. The brakes on our bikes didn't really work, but as Johannes pointed out, brakes are overrated. It added to the fun, after all.

It was early morning, and for the most part, we were the only tourists around. It could have been due to the rain that had only just stopped as we arrived, but this seems like a far less visited destination on the tourist tract which I always find immediately attractive.

A few magical things happened during my time there: first, a group of monks who were touring the temple were only a few steps ahead of us and perfect for photographing. I caught one of them taking a photo of me, surprised that we had the same objective. He then asked if we could take one together, which I found to be pretty touching.

Next, at the statue of King Ramkhamhaeng, a cute old Thai man helped Louise and I read one of the ancient chants. He quietly said the words and we immediately repeated them.

Then he beckoned us over to the other side of the shrine, said a little prayer, and applied gold leaf to our foreheads right where the third eye sits.

Jaded, I figured he might hold his hand out for a donation thereafter, but he did no such thing. He gave us both hugs and sent us on our way.

We were like mini local celebrities with children cheerfully yelling hello as they saw us biking by. It felt like Kratie all over again.

After a lovely day of biking around and enjoying the ruins

and giant Buddha statues, I bid Johannes and Louise goodbye and headed back to my guesthouse. I made a wrong turn walking back and started to get a bit lost. Luckily a friendly local could tell I must be heading in the wrong direction and offered me a ride, gratis, on his motorbike.

Perhaps it's due to the lower influx of tourists in Sukhothai, or perhaps the locals are simply friendlier here, but I felt extremely welcomed in this little pocket of Thailand. I can tell they're not tired of us tourists here, yet. They still welcome us with open arms.

I'm very glad to have seen this for myself. I'm glad I followed the word-of-mouth advice and that I left that guidebook behind in the car on the way to the airport after all. It was the best mistake I could have made.

22

December 16, 2012

Day 80

On a warm night in Chiang Mai a couple of weeks ago, I met up with a few fellow bloggers for a night out at the street food stalls and met Yvonne, a German blogger with a gorgeous back tattoo. We got on the topic of tattoos and I admitted to her that I had made an appointment to get some ink twice and backed out twice, too, deciding that what I thought I wanted ultimately lacked enough meaning to carry on my body forever.

Then she told me about the magical monk tattoo – a spiritual Sak Yant that was chosen and applied by a Buddhist monk based on what he thought the recipient needed. I felt like I might have finally found the perfect tattoo for me – something that had a deeper meaning than any other tattoo could possibly possess.

The Sak Yant tattoo at Wat Bang Phra, 55km outside of Bangkok, is performed by a famous monk named Luang Pi Nunn in exchange for a small donation of flowers, cigarettes, and incense that is then recycled and sold again in order to keep the wat afloat. In exchange, the monk considers which of the 80-something Sak Yant symbols he wishes to apply. Without any prior discussion, he gets to work.

His tools include a long bamboo pole and ink made from snake's venom, Chinese charcoal ink, and palm oil.

We made plans to get the tattoo together, and this time I vowed not to back out.

Flash-forward several weeks: I awoke today at the ripe hour of 4:30am to meet up with Yvonne to get our tattoos done.

Oh, who am I kidding? I was too excited and scared to sleep at all.

Aware of just how popular Wat Bang Phra is amongst locals to get their Sak Yant tattoos, we knew we had to catch the 6am bus that leaves from the Victory Monument in Bangkok in order to be first in line.

We got to the temple seamlessly after alighting the bus and catching a delightful moto-taxi ride through rice paddies as the red sun was rising.

We arrived at the wat slightly unsure of what to do next. A little Thai man roused from his slumber and helped us purchase our offerings for 65 baht then handed us pink envelopes to put additional offerings into. In all, I donated 120 baht (USD $4 – not bad for a tattoo!).

We settled into the room and I somehow ended up at the front of the queue. There were about fifteen of us in the room – locals, Yvonne, and myself. I had wanted Yvonne to go first, given she already has tattoos and therefore would naturally be less anxious than I would be.

But the monk beckoned me and there was no turning back. I crawled into position, bent over a pyramid pillow, and dug my nails into my arm so that I would be able to focus my pain on another area. Two men on either side of me held my skin taut while the monk, a piece of paper separating his hand from my skin, as he can't touch female flesh, dipped his long bamboo needle into ink.

The tapping began. As expected, we had not discussed what he was going to do. We had not selected a precise location – he just went for it. I knew from the beginning that I had to put faith in his design choice and placement based on his interpretation of my aura – based on his opinion of what blessing I needed most. I knew that I would have no say in what tattoo I got nor where it would go.

Ten minutes and roughly 3,000 strikes later, I had a new tattoo. I had expected the pain to be out of this world, but in reality it wasn't so bad. It was therapeutic in a way.

As he finished, he blew on the tattoo to breathe power into it as he chanted a blessing. Then he moved onto Yvonne unto whom he bestowed the same tattoo.

When hers was finished, we left the room and excitedly took pictures of each other's tattoos so that we could see our fresh ink for the first time. Both looked amazing. He had given us the Hah Taew – the sacred five lines.

Though each monk has his own version of the Hah Taew, it generally bestows a blessing of loving kindness, lifelong success, charm, good luck, and protection against bad luck and evil spirits.

This was easily one of the most magical and enduring parts of my journey so far. I will forever remember the beauty of the day and the uplifting feeling of the blessing. After all, how can I forget? I'll carry this reminder on my shoulder forever.

Yvonne and I made our way back to Bangkok, our bodies

buzzing with adrenaline. I'd never felt this way before and she ensured me it was the feeling you get after you get a new tattoo – smiling from ear to ear.

I felt like I was on cloud nine. Everything seemed perfect except one little thing seemed to be off. Joshua wasn't answering my texts, and I hated that on a day that was so special to me he was suddenly absent.

We'd had a tough time in the days prior. He didn't like that I was off getting a tattoo without him. I thought it was strange that he was bothered by it. He didn't like that from time to time when we were chatting, I signed off without saying goodbye first. I figured he would have understood that sometimes, a bus pulls into the terminal, or something suddenly comes up when you're traveling and you simply don't have time to say goodbye. I thought our conversations were ongoing but to him, I was off having an adventure and he was stuck at home stressing about what I was doing.

He was bothered that I still spoke to guys from back home and hung out with and even shared rooms with guy friends while I traveled. I still didn't get the problem. I was just friends with them and nothing sinister was happening. He mistrusted me from the beginning and it was starting to feel like he was turning out to be quite controlling.

"What's up with you?" I prodded via text.

"Nothing I expect you'll care much about," he cryptically replied.

I wanted clarification and called him, upset that he was making the day about him when it had been such a special experience for me.

A friend of his from back home had heard his side of the

story and suggested to him that perhaps I wasn't a good use of his time. I was off being selfish and wasn't investing enough in the relationship, he said.

"Well of course," I replied, "I'm traveling right now–this is supposed to be the trip of a lifetime!"

I thought he understood that.

With that, he said he would probably not be able to come in January and wanted us to take a few days of silence from each other.

I was left stunned. Where was that guy who was so funny, patient, and kind when he was with me in Laos? He seemed to be so carefree and understanding.

Thankfully, tonight I will meet back up with my girlfriends from Pai and we're heading south to the islands. I need a break from everything, and the ocean is calling. I suppose things will work out the way they're meant to eventually, but I can't help but feel incredibly sad at this loss. I don't know exactly what I've lost, though. It's either the vision of something that never really existed or a guy who's still in there somewhere, harboring my safe dream of a secure future with him.

23

December 17-23, 2012

Days 81-87

The past few days have been a blur. I'm so happy to be back with my girlfriends, but I'm finding the Thai islands to be a mixture of debauchery and seediness.

I've met a few people here who say that even just four years ago it was a completely different vibe here. The beaches were quieter and calmer, the locals were friendlier, and it wasn't all about partying all night.

Now, Koh Tao, a diving island in Southern Thailand, seems to be reserved for flaming jump ropes and two-for-one buckets of entirely-too-strong alcohol. While I love a good dance party, this cesspool of casual sex and booze isn't my scene at all and I completely empathize with the locals who are watching as their beautiful island slowly but surely succumbs to 20-something international kids on Christmas break. We spend the kind of cash in two weeks that a local is happy to make in a few months, and it's cheap to us. We're trashing this place, and I'm disgusted, too.

Beyond that, my heart is torn to shreds. Joshua has waffled between wanting to talk to me and missing me and threatening to break things off completely. It's like I'm a marionette and he's pulling the strings. He knows it and he's wielding his power like a dictator. I hate how much control he has over my emotions and the situation, and I'm even more frustrated with myself for letting it get to this point.

I just keep thinking of the guy I met in Vang Vieng. He was so perfect back then and I made the mistake of latching onto a vision of a perfect future with him. It's all too much for me and I'm not sure how to handle it, but I do know that I don't want to be in this party atmosphere anymore. I'm done.

Christmas and New Year's are coming up and I'm not sure what to do, but I'm not spending it with Joshua, and I'm not spending it at a full moon party, either – my replacement plan. I need some solitude and quick, or I just might go crazy.

I guess this is what my friend meant when she said the beautiful beginning wouldn't last forever. I completely understand her now, but I wish I didn't.

24

December 24, 2012

Day 88

I said goodbye to my girlfriends today. They've mostly paired off with handsome boys, and they're otherwise occupied enjoying the islands. I know that I'm being kind of a Debbie Downer, and the best thing that I can do right now is go seek some solitude.

A random person in the dorm the other day on Koh Tao told me that I should still head to Koh Phangan and that there are quiet and beautiful places on that island that almost nobody knows about or visits. One is called Bottle Beach, and it's not even accessible by road. I took his advice and now here I am, in a little bungalow on my own, on a very quiet and sleepy stretch of beach that seems the polar opposite to the other side of the island where the full moon party will be in full swing in less than a week for New Year's.

"Kristin! You bring the waves! Yesterday, no have. But you come, and today, they follow you."

This is what Sam, the cheerful Thai owner of the bungalow I'm staying in (Smile Bungalows), informed me of as I settled down on the wooden deck for breakfast.

I shrugged and said, "Oh, sorry!" but in reality, I like it

better this way. The placid waters of Cambodia and Koh Tao were quite nice, but, being from California, I naturally have an appreciation for waves, as well.

I sat and watched them roll in and out all morning. This is such a nice contrast to the madness that Koh Tao turned out to be. I had hoped it might be somewhat like Otres and the island of Koh Rong in Cambodia – a diver's paradise. But in reality, it was an intense party scene with end of the world ragers, buckets, and aggressively intoxicated backpackers. I fear those days are ahead for Koh Rong, as well, but I certainly hope not.

Bottle Beach has not disappointed. It only has four sets of bungalows dotting the beach and is nestled in its own secluded cove. I'm back to the cold shower, bamboo bungalow, mosquito net, lack of power during the day, no Wi-Fi zone that I have come to realize I absolutely adore and crave.

On the deck where I spend most of the day reading and reflecting, I met a middle-aged English expat who has lived here for "nine years," he said. Assuming he meant Thailand in general, I was impressed, but then he explained that he has lived in the same bungalow, just like the one I am staying in, at this very guesthouse, for all of those nine years.

Yes, he showed up and liked it enough to stay, right here, on this teeny, tiny beach, without power for most of the day not to even mention the lack of cell signal or Internet, for nine years.

He said something that resonated: sometimes, something happens that jolts you to reality and causes you to reevaluate what's important in life and what you really want out of it. For him, it was his brother passing away at only 35, leaving behind Porsches and Lotuses. What good did it do him to work his whole life only to die before he could enjoy it? What worth did his earthly possessions have if they could not follow him to the grave?

He believes that most people who travel long-term had a moment like this, a shock to the head, as he called it. I know I did. It happened when I was sitting in my BMW, a Louis Vuitton purse next to me and several deals at the firm under letter of intent. I felt trapped and thought to myself, "Why don't these things make me happy? The ads and magazine advertorials always made it seem like having glamorous things brought joy, but it doesn't at all. It brings nothing."

He went all around the world looking for a new place to settle and decided on Bottle Beach. He added that most of the people he sees here stay for a month, or they stay briefly then they come back again and stay for a while. Most visitors who are here right now have been here before and wanted to return.

That, to me, says a lot about the place. Perhaps there is still a small corner of the Thai islands that is pure, unchanged, and can remain peaceful, far from buckets and mindless drunkards. I hope that's in the cards for Bottle Beach.

Sometimes, something magical happens when you travel: you remember exactly why you're doing it, and you're so happy and present in that moment. Sometimes it's the people you meet; sometimes it's the places you're at.

Sometimes, it's both.

25

December 31, 2012 – January 11, 2013

Days 95-106

Last week during a starry night on Koh Tao, I was lying on a wooden deck, staring up at the stars as party revelers danced away at the bar to my right. I was tired of dancing, I was tired of reckless tourists — I was tired of the whole Thai island backpacker party scene in general.

A Finnish guy whose name escapes me now asked if he could watch the stars with me. I reluctantly agreed, hoping he wasn't like the rest of the guys on this island: overly eager to get in the pants of anything that walks and has boobs.

To my delight, he felt like I did and was simply tired of the parties. He spoke of a place where one could meditate for ten days, a Buddhist monastery in the forest where the attendees don't speak, use technology, or even read books. They just meditate.

The next morning, I woke up and began my research.

The retreat would begin on December 31st, meaning I would miss celebrating New Year's. I had booked the Full Moon and New Years parties on Koh Phangan, but quickly decided that they weren't for me given how annoyed I already was by the comparatively tamer party scene on Koh Tao. I canceled my reservations that day.

Flash-forward several days and I'd made my way to Bottle Beach and then back to the mainland to reach Chiaya, the nearest town to Wat Suan Mokkh. It was the highest-rated and coincidentally closest meditation retreat I could find in Thailand. It's also the most traditional, without any frills or an expensive price tag. The timing was perfect. Here's how it went:

Eve of December 31 – The Silence Begins

I sat silently on a small mat over a coconut sack on the sand in the open-air meditation hall at Suan Mokkh Forest Monastery surrounded by 40 other women and about 50 men as the fireworks of the celebration in the nearby town of Chaiya exploded and boomed in the distance. I smiled to myself – I knew I had chosen the best way to ring in the New Year.

4 AM on January 1 – Wake up Bell

I awoke with a start on my concrete bed as the bell rang out over the grounds of Suan Mokkh. I made my way to the water well we all shared and washed my face and brushed my teeth silently. I was not to utter a word for the next ten days. I almost blew it when I shrieked in my room, afraid my mosquito net brushing against my arm in the darkness was a scorpion – we had been warned we might encounter them in our rooms.

I did not put on makeup – we vowed not to. I did not apply perfume – another vow we took. I dressed conservatively, grabbed my headlamp, and made my way back to the meditation hall for the morning reading. It was a passage by Jiddu Krishnamurti about making use of the early morning hours. How fitting; crickets were chirping and birds were just beginning to sing.

4:45 AM – Sitting Meditation

I sat and tried to pay attention to my breathing. There was no way this was happening. My mind, slippery as it was, had no intention of focus. I took a mental trip to the previous summer at Burning Man, returned to the beach back home, headed back to Vang Vieng…

No! Focus, Kristin! Ok, breathing, in, out, in, out… I wonder what Joshua's up to? No! He's probably sleeping because it's 4am. Breathe in…breathe out…Oh, that's a nice pair of hippie pants she has, wonder where she got them?

Ding! The bell rang and it was time for an hour and a half of morning yoga.

For the first time, I did sun salutations as the sun rose.

7 AM – Dhamma Talk and More Meditation

An old Thai monk with striking blue eyes sat at the front of the hall and repeated phrases that would come to define my struggles with meditation over the next few days – we had to let go of our sense of self. We had to let go of 'me' and 'mine' in order to let go of desire to find the true path to meditation. In other words, we couldn't want it and we couldn't expect it.

It's pretty hard for a Westerner, raised the way we are, to grasp this.

We sat in meditation for another 45 minutes after his talk. I was lost in my subconscious, going over past arguments, having future conversations in my head, writing mentally, thinking of what this entry might hold; anything but taming my bucking bronco of a mind.

Ding! It was time for breakfast.

8 AM – Breakfast and Chores

Our breakfast meal was the introduction to what the rest of them would be for the next eight days: brown rice porridge with various specks of vegetables with leafy greens and cucumber to stir inside. Some small bananas served as the dessert (the final two days there was just one meal – no breakfast).

My chore turned out to be raking the sand in the meditation hall. I came to love my chore. The act was therapeutic and so symbolic to me that I was lucky enough to lovingly comb and flatten the sand in the very hall where, in the coming days, I'd have profound realizations about myself, my relationships, what I wanted out of my future, and what was really important to me in life. Moreover, this hall would be the very place where I'd finally meditate for the first time (on day four, for only 10 minutes, but it's a start!)

It sure beat the hell out of cleaning toilets or footbaths.

10 AM – Dhamma Talk

This talk usually consisted of learning more about Buddhism which should have come as a shocker to nobody considering we were sitting in a Buddhist monastery.

I came to find a lot of stock in what we were learning, some of the most pertinent of which was the urging to let go of the past and not angst over the future. We were instructed to be present. This is much more easily said than done, of course. The keys to happiness are, however, in being mindful, as it turns out.

11 AM – Walking Meditation

I had never seen walking meditation before which consists of taking about five full seconds per step. I watched as my fellow meditators lumbered about like zombies around the forested grounds of the wat looking dazed in the eyes.

At the very least I was becoming that much more prepared for the zombie apocalypse.

I stole the moment to find my refuge amongst a forest of coconut trees. I noticed things about the trees I had never seen before like the perfectly folded palm fronds and the geometrical nature of the rings around the trunks. I stared at them and actually appreciated them for the first time.

I watched a colony of ants for twenty minutes, fascinated by the organization. I found a scorpion and followed it for another twenty minutes, absolutely mesmerized by the way it walked. I would have never done this otherwise.

11:45 AM – Sitting Meditation

My mind wandered back to the previous summer at Burning Man:

No! Focus! I wonder what Joshua's doing now? Shhh! Quiet, you stubborn mind. Is that a mosquito? I will annihilate it! Oh wait, I took a vow not to take away breath. Shit.

Ding! The bell rang out again.

12:30 PM – Lunch and Chores

Lunch was our second and final meal of the day. It was a mild vegetable curry over brown rice, some sort of tofu salad, and a banana coconut milk dessert. Over the days, it would vary but would always keep the same theme: a vegetable curry, a coconut milk dessert, and some other surprise of noodles, tofu, or papaya salad.

I really came to love lunchtime.

I raked the sand once again.

I slathered on DEET.

2:30 PM – Dhamma Talk

My very favorite speaker, the English monk, took this time slot today and each day moving forward. He spoke of how to rid our lives of dukkha (suffering) by letting go. He used examples of dukkha from his own life prior to becoming a monk. The reflection on his past mirrored many of our present situations of daily confusion and lack of mindfulness.

He helped me to understand.

3:30 PM – More Meditation

Walking, standing, sitting meditation. My slippery mind remained slippery, so I finally went with it and focused on a few things that had been bothering me. I worked them out in my head and felt better. Over the following days this would continue until my mind, with no books, pencils, cell phone, speaking with other humans, or computer to occupy it, I got tired of thinking and finally submitted to paying attention to my in-and-out breathing.

5 PM – Chanting and Loving Kindness

We chanted from a book of praises. Just one verse still sticks with me now:

> "One ought to not long for what has passed away,
>
> Nor be anxious over things that are yet to come.

The past has left us, the future has not arrived."

We breathed loving kindness to those who we loved and those who had wronged us, made peace with our pasts, and enveloped the world in our puppies and rainbows feelings.

Given we were not supposed to kill mosquitoes, this was the hardest part of the day for me as the sun usually set during loving kindness time and the little monsters came out in droves.

I watched as one of my fellow meditators clapped her hands and killed a mosquito in the row in front of me, boldly breaking the rule not to kill any living beings. I resolved to direct my loving kindness towards her for saving me another bite.

6:30 PM – Tea and Bathing Time

This was not tea, as caffeine was not allowed, but rather a welcome cup (or in my case, three) of steaming hot chocolate.

I followed this up with splashing cold water from the shared well onto my sarong-covered body. This was how we bathed. I yelped in spite of myself at the first bucket of water – 'twas a cold surprise.

7:30 PM – Sitting, Group Walking, then Sitting Meditation

The evening culminated with more meditation. We walked as a group around the two ponds – the men in one row and the women in another. Dim candles lit our way as we paraded, ever so mindfully and silently, under the stars in the forest monastery in the small town of Chaiya, Southern Thailand.

9:30 PM – Lights Out

I ventured back to my dorm and checked the area for scorpions and centipedes. Satisfied that there were none and somewhat thankful for the spiders in my room (after all, they were not required to practice loving kindness towards mosquitoes), I laid back on my concrete bed, covered myself with my mosquito net, and drifted off to sleep rather easily.

The days that followed were much the same. The meditation was difficult – in fact it's one of the most difficult things I've ever done. However, it's also one of the most rewarding things I've done, and the benefits are still with me now.

I finally got my cell phone and belongings back at the end of the retreat and checked my phone. There was a message from Joshua. I wasn't sure how to handle it, but the lines of communication seemed to be open again. He asked me to come to Melbourne and give us a try.

On one hand, I'd hoped he'd say something like that; on the other, I half wished he'd disappear from my life completely and just let me be on my way.

I left the meditation with a clear head but just one text clouded it again with question after question. What's the right move? Should I change my plans and head to Australia almost a year earlier than initially planned? Will I have regrets no matter which path I choose?

What should I do?

26

January 17 – 21

Days 112-116

It's been a while, hasn't it? I've been pretty quiet, I know. Ever since right before the meditation I've been battling with my ears. To be more specific, I've been battling with an unwelcome guest that has taken up residence in my ears. It's been three weeks and I've seen three doctors, each of whom has prescribed a different antibiotic. It seems I have a persistent middle-ear infection.

I spent a few days between bed and the sand in Khao Lak just up the coast in Southwestern Thailand, unable to do much other than lie there and pray my inflamed tonsils away. The insides of my ears were screaming and the infection has worked its way down to my throat as well. Each night has consisted of five or so hours of sleep. I've been pretty much bed-ridden and finally broke down and rented a room with air conditioning because it's so hot, I was feeling feverish in the room with just a fan.

Please, pleeeease be gone. Please don't be what I think you are, I pleaded with my body as I tried in vain to equalize my ears.

I had booked a six-day, 18-tank, live-aboard dive trip in the

Similan Islands which was rumored to be some of the best diving in the world. I was so excited. I had expected this to be one of the highlights of my travels in Southeast Asia.

The day of the dive came and I couldn't ignore it anymore; I had to see a doctor – the fourth doctor I would see in the span of three weeks.

"You have a middle ear infection; at this point, it's chronic. No diving for you for at least five days," he told me. Crushed, I canceled my diving trip and whipped out a map to see where I might head to next.

Krabi sounded good; and wasn't too far away, so I jumped on the next bus out.

I had heard good things about Railay, near Krabi, and therefore set my sights on that as a final destination. However, on the long-tail boat over, we passed a seemingly underdeveloped stretch of beach, nearly devoid of much apart from misty skies and wooden bungalows.

"What's that?" I wondered. I landed on Railay which was full of Russian tourists and a few air-conditioned resorts and immediately headed back to the water taxi and asked to be taken to the other beach which he told me was Tonsai.

We pulled up and the electricity suddenly buzzed on. The stretch of beach with wooden decks over the water and reggae beats lit up and I felt a sigh of relief. I had found the spot I'd stick to for the duration of my time in Thailand.

Tonsai is the type of place that pulls you in. Most people who visit end up staying here for several weeks, if not months, without even meaning to or planning on it. It's where those iconic rocks rise up out of the water seemingly out of nowhere and long-tail boats with flowers in front for good luck bob up and down in the water, reminding you that you're in Thailand. These types of places always seem to steal my heart.

My days were spent lazily wading through the water, laying on the wooden decks, staring at the long-tail boats, and reading Jack Kerouac novels.

Though not particularly easy with a middle ear infection, as it threw off my equilibrium, I tried out one of the more popular activities on Tonsai – slack-line walking, which is kind of like tightrope walking but on a thicker line and closer to the ground. The more skilled 'slack-liners' can jump from line to line, balance on one leg, and lie down on the line only to push themselves back up without falling. It's impressive, to say the least.

The other favorite activity in Tonsai is rock climbing, given the near-vertical cliffs that line the beach. Each evening, base jumpers whoop as they hurl themselves from the tops of the cliffs to the beach below. When not hanging or jumping from cliffs, most people kayak or swim in the beautiful blue sea.

But me? I laid on the wooden decks of my favorite coffee shop and drank chai teas churned out by an awesomely tattooed local who wielded a mortar and pestle.

Every day when I got up to leave, he'd ask, "When are you coming back?"

Each day I said, "I'll see you tomorrow!" extending my stay that much longer and writing off Koh Phi Phi as my penciled-in finale of Thailand.

Every now and then I sat up to survey the beautiful sea in front of me. I even caught a sunset or two.

I finished the very last day of my two-ish months in Thailand right on the beach in Tonsai. It took a lot of searching, but as it turns out there are still beautiful, unspoiled beaches in Thailand, thank goodness!

Perhaps the ear infection was what the doctor ordered, after all.

Tonsai, I'm coming back someday, but for now, I have a flight to Melbourne to catch.

Part 5

Australia: The Land that Arrived Too Soon

27

January 23, 2013

Day 118

I landed in Melbourne and already I feel strange. When I landed in Bangkok it felt so right, but sitting here in Australia I can't say I feel that sense of security. I thought coming here would solve the conflict in my heart, but it seems to have exacerbated it.

I haven't let on that I feel this way. Joshua is none the wiser, and I'm sure it must just be nerves. We had a tumultuous few months leading up to this and, after periods of not talking and him threatening, I managed to get back in his good graces and was sure that moving here to make this work was the answer.

Perhaps that was naïve.

Melbourne is a very cool city and I liked it immediately upon arriving here. It was already dark when Joshua picked me up from the airport with a bouquet of flowers and a tear glistening in his eye. As I sat on the back of his motorbike when we rode into the city, I stared up at the stars and spotted the Southern Cross constellation for the first time. For some reason I found it comforting.

The city has a San Francisco vibe. What I mean by that is it's artsy, laid-back, and unfortunately, insanely expensive. I can definitely see myself here, though. It's safe, has all kinds of interesting neighborhoods to explore and, most importantly, is on the coast.

The only thing I'm just not sure about is my heart.

28

February 1, 2013

Day 127

Since neither of us can afford the insanely high rent around here, which runs at around $400 per week for a one-bedroom apartment, I've moved in with Joshua and his family. They're absolutely lovely people and I couldn't be more thankful for their generosity and hospitality.

I also found a job fairly easily. I'm working at a mall called Chadstone's at a high-end footwear store. They pay me $23 per hour to sell shoes. It's easy and people are nice, but I can't help but feel like I'm back on the hamster wheel. I know I should check my ego at the door, but I keep feeling like it's a step backwards to have left investment banking to work in the service industry like I did when I was younger.

I also have a sinking feeling in the pit of my stomach that I keep trying to ignore. It's the same feeling I had at the end of my last relationship, which wasn't so long ago, so I remember it well: something isn't right.

If this is meant to be the start of something wonderful and beautiful, then why do I feel so unsafe, unstable, and fearful? I'm incredibly stifled and feel like I can't do much of anything without Joshua wanting to put a leash on me and make all of my decisions for me.

Each day I feel less sure about us. I notice that the carefree guy who laughed so openly and was so generous with his love, time, and money is suddenly a ball of stress who was hoping I'd use my savings for "us" while in Melbourne. My travel dreams are slipping further and further away from me and the walls are closing in. I feel trapped in a place that most people absolutely adore.

My biggest realization is that I never knew the real Joshua at all, and I fantasize about buying a plane ticket back to Asia and disappearing without a word or a trace. It's terrible to think this way, isn't it? I keep suppressing those feelings, sure that we're just going through some growing pains.

My heartstrings still keep me here, imprisoned by my own delusions of what we could be, what I thought we were, and who I thought he was. It has occurred to me now that I never spent time with him in a real-life setting with stress and the pressures of school, work, and money. He was just in vacation mode, so no wonder he was so carefree. I took a giant leap of faith sight unseen. I was a foolish girl, but lust means rose-colored glasses and a diminished sense of reason.

Australia is also pillaging my wallet quickly. The Australian dollar is stronger than the US dollar at the moment, and I'm flabbergasted that a plate of just eggs and toast the other morning cost me $12. How is that even possible? Just for eggs? I had to pick my jaw up off the floor and Joshua acted annoyed that I'd said too loudly that it was way too expensive.

I think he figured I should have the savings to support all of this from my old job. I'm starting to realize he expects I'll pay for a lot of things for both of us now as he promises to pay for them later when he graduates from his master's program. The only thing is I'm seeing less and less of a "later" for us as I discover more things about him that I didn't see before. Again, I don't vocalize this. I just think these thoughts to myself and then immediately try to replace those thoughts with positive ones. I'm here now; I need to give this a real try before I give up, right?

29

March 20, 2013

Day 174

Things are spinning out of control. The other day I caught Joshua snooping on my Facebook, demanding that I stop talking to old male acquaintances of mine, drawing conclusions that aren't there.

Little things his friends have said when he wasn't around lead me to believe we've both been doing things perhaps the other wouldn't have been happy to see while we were apart, but long distance takes its toll that way. He points the finger, but won't admit to any wrongdoing.

It's not that we didn't have good times when we were together, at least in the beginning. He took me to the botanical gardens and we laid in the sun, counting the leaves on the massive trees. We explored and laughed and cuddled in bed for hours. Those moments made me think that there was still some good in there. It was a garden, and I had to water the flowers if I wanted it to flourish.

Yet, little by little, our lack of money took its toll. The stress of school got to him, and at the same time, homesickness hit me really hard. Around that time, he stated that he can't handle me traveling anywhere without him ever again. He doesn't feel that he can trust me and for his own sake needs me to be around.

This is the last straw and I need to plan an exit strategy.

I'm going to have to stick it out for the next couple of weeks and revisit when flights are more reasonably priced. At the moment, I need to keep earning at the shoe shop so that I can afford to leave.

I can't believe I ever let it get to this point, but there's no use crying over spilled milk now. I just need to find a way to intelligently move forward.

30

March 25, 2013

Day 179

I made a mistake by following my heart.

I'm naked, picking up the pieces of who I was.

I'd decided at the beginning of this trip that I needed to be single for at least the next year of my life. I had just ended a four-year relationship, and the weight of it had yet to fully hit me. I yearned for freedom and it was so good at first.

It was like every day during my first two months of traveling were in high-definition, smell and taste-o-vision, intensified bliss. I felt freer than a bird. I was higher than any drug could have taken me. To say the feeling was ecstasy would be doing it a disservice.

Life was everything I had always wanted it to be.

Then Joshua happened, and that's when it all started and picked up momentum and became a roller coaster, and before I knew it, I had lost all control. The wheel had been passed from me to someone else. I lost myself.

My friend Emma from Thailand was never a fan of Joshua. She hated how he jerked me around and, quite logically I see now, told me that I was rushing into it and hadn't given myself enough time to get over my last relationship. She cautioned me against filling that void with another relationship rather than self-discovery and self-love. She was right, but I was in too deep to hear her.

Two weeks ago when I was at work at the shoe shop, I got a call from Joshua towards the end of my shift. I could tell from the echo that he was clearly in a room in a house, not outside on his motorbike.

"It sounds like you're still at home," I said to him.

He was supposed to pick me up from work so that I could head to another interview. I was going to pick up another job to help get more money in, either to support us both, or to buy a plane ticket ASAP. I wasn't sure yet.

"Yeah, I'm not coming," he said.

He ended the relationship right there, over the phone. When I headed back to the house he wasn't home, but his parents were. It was horribly awkward, but I packed up what little I had and called my friend Chrissy whom I know from Pai. She graciously came to pick up the pieces of me that were left and offered me a place to stay. I've been sleeping on the spare mattress in her room for the past two weeks. I really don't know what I would have done without her and her incredibly kind roommates who haven't minded having me around. On the contrary, they've welcomed me with open arms.

In this battle for heart preservation and emotional dominance it appears that I lost. The winner is the quickest one to the finish line, and I slowed down to let him pass even though I'd been contemplating a breakup almost since I arrived in Melbourne. It was always a game, and he always held the cards, and, for that, I feel weak and foolish.

I guess I kept thinking about those relationships where someone knew someone whose cousin met Mr. Right and lived happily ever after. But this isn't a fairy tale and I'm not Cinderella. She wore glass heels and I'm not even willing to wear regular heels. She rode around in a giant gourd, and as anyone who has ever carved a pumpkin knows, it must've been moist and stringy in there, but she put up with it for Prince Charming. If you ask me, he should have just loved her for who she was, rags and all. She shouldn't have had to pretend.

That's what I've been doing for the past month – pretending like I'm fine with working instead of exploring new corners of the world. Acting like I wasn't choking from the overbearing person I was with even though I was suffocating and pretending like I didn't wholly regret leaving my adventure behind even though it plagued me every day. In the end, it wasn't enough.

I know this is a blessing in disguise, but it doesn't mean my chest doesn't hurt when I breathe from the weight of the conflicted emotions.

It's my last night in Melbourne. Tonight Chrissy and I went for a walk in St. Kilda, a hipster neighborhood of Melbourne, and I noticed a thick line of smog on the horizon. It reminded me of the smog back home. It reminded me of everything I had intentionally left behind.

I didn't take enough time for me and I see that now. Just like every other time, I'll pick up the pieces, and I'll move on.

Asia, my darling, I'm coming back to you. Thank you so much for waiting for me. I always knew you would.

Part 6

Thailand: The Revisited Land of Redemption

31

April 15, 2013

Day 200

Most people know the feeling of déjà vu. It's when you can't quite place it, but you know you've felt exactly that way before in another time and another place.

There's an opposite to this feeling called jamais vu. It's when you go back to the same place but nothing about it is familiar, and you feel like nothing but strangers surround you.

That's how it felt to return here to Tonsai beach in Thailand, the very place I'd fell so hard in love with and departed from over two months ago.

The sun hung low in the sky as I walked across the salty water, avoiding submerged rocks and gazing out at the rock climbers and slack-line walkers on the cliffs around the beach. I trudged through the calm, knee-deep waves, still at least a good 50 meters from shore, as the long-tail boat could only come so close given that the tide was out and the beach is known for its boulders.

I reached the sand as reggae played in the distance just as it did before, and locals called out, "how are you?" as I walked by. This is the same beach I visited only a few months ago, but one thing is immediately apparent – it is much calmer and quieter.

It's low season now, and there is just a third to a quarter of the amount of people lazing about as there was the last time I was here.

The tattoo shop is shuttered. The bar I had a fabulous curry at last time now only serves drinks. A resulting piece of good news: the bungalows I was hoping to stay in actually have room this time, and at a lower rate than before.

A rock climber sat with me this evening while I ate a dinner of pineapple rice. Everyone who walked by seemed to know him. He had been there for a few weeks and could barely imagine how it was during high season. "A zoo, I reckon," he said. I confirmed that it was, indeed, a happening place. I can't imagine anyone knowing each person who walked by back then, as he did.

Some things are the same – the beautiful rocks that rise up like giants and frame the beach still tower over me. The same guy calls out, "Where are you going? Where you been?" and the fire dancers still light up the beach at night.

I can't help but be struck by something unnerving, though. It was more beautiful to me before, but back then, it was new.

There is no reason for this. Daily, I sit with new friends who are here because I told them about how cool this place is. They thank me profusely and talk about how it's the most gorgeous place they've been to in Thailand. The leaves are turning red, and monkeys play in the distance. If I can't appreciate this, can I appreciate anything?

The old familiar feelings of traveling through Southeast Asia that initially had me so enamored have returned somewhat, but at the same time, everything feels different to me now. I want to be my old self again, but I'm still trying to find her.

Perhaps it is I who is the stranger back in the very same familiar place.

Slowly but surely, I will gain my perspective back. I'll be that girl who loves and laughs curiously and without reserve again. I won't let my scars keep me from living openly and spontaneously. It'll just take some time to get there, and that's okay.

32

April 17, 2013

Day 202

My friend Matt showed up yesterday and brought an energy with him that I needed. He's also a travel blogger, and we met several months ago at a conference in Colorado. He's tall and kind-hearted with big blue eyes and a sense of adventure.

Until he showed up, I planned to generally be a lazy bum drinking chai tea and reading books all day. I was content to sit on the deck of Chill Out Bar with my Kindle, glancing up every now and then at the amazing view, and maybe walk to Mama's Chicken stand every so often to stuff my face with some curry and pat myself on the back for discovering the amazing coconut milk and Oreo shake combination.

But when Matt and I realized we were geographically quite proximate, he turned his course south and came to hang out, completely ruining my grand plans of idleness.

"I heard about this really cool lagoon in Railay. Want to walk over there tomorrow?" he asked.

I heard 'walk' and figured it would be a leisurely stroll, so I agreed.

Railay is the beach directly next to Tonsai. As I mentioned before, I find it a bit too resorty for my tastes (read: there are not enough people with dreadlocks and not nearly enough reggae music on loop), but I was happy to check it out for the afternoon. We made the 15-minute climb through a tiny jungle and some rocks on the beach and, sweat already permeating my being, continued from Railay West to Railay East through the resorts and shops. Following the signs, we finally stopped in front of a stake in the ground with an arrow pointing straight up reading "trail to lagoon."

It led to a muddy set of rocks with ropes dangling down – ropes that were clearly needed to scale the rocks upwards.

I shot Matt a glance, "I suppose I'll be climbing in Railay after all!"

"Just so you know, it's really muddy up there," said a passer-by. I elected to remove my shoes and my in-the-tubing tank top from Laos, as I prize that thing more than a rational person should, and pronounced myself ready. We quickly got to work climbing hand and foot.

Several groups of climbers passed by us on the way down, exclaiming, "Oh! So difficult! So muddy!"

We thought surely they were just messing with us.

"I didn't make it to the lagoon. It's pretty much a vertical drop beyond the lookout point…barefooted?! You're doing it barefooted?" exclaimed an Aussie passing us on the way down.

"Better for gripping," I replied. He nodded skeptically and continued on his way.

After 25 minutes or so of fairly reasonable climbing we reached the lookout point where it seemed most people ended their hikes and turned back for Railay.

We stood there for about five minutes to appreciate the

beauty of the lookout point before turning back to the trail and setting our sights on the lagoon. We figured we had made it that far, and we were certainly not turning back.

As we made our way closer to the lagoon, the rumors turned out to be true: the trail, appearing to be something out of *Jurassic Park*, turned quite muddy and became a vertical rock climb, sans gear, to the bottom. Our tools for scaling the rock wall were our hands, bare feet, and some muddy ropes hanging from the top.

Matt was a champ. He took each climb first then told me where to place my feet when it was my turn to head down. We scaled four steep declines, sometimes dangling only by a rope, before finally seeing some jade water in the distance.

By the time we reached the lagoon, we decided to embrace the mud and headed to the cave to write in mud on the walls, smear it all over our faces, and wash it right off in the lagoon like some sort of swanky spa afternoon thereafter.

The climb back up seemed a bit easier since we'd already done it once and could see what we were doing a bit more easily, though it did require a fair amount more upper-body strength.

We rewarded ourselves with coconut milk and Oreo shakes when we got back, because can you think of anything better on a hot day on a secluded beach in the south of Thailand?

We followed that up with a few rounds of Jenga at the Sunset Bar and a couple of celebratory Singha beers. It would be my last night in Tonsai as I've gone ahead and rebooked my diving trip that I missed thanks to the ear infection back in January. I can't wait to get back under the water again.

Thanks, Matt, for encouraging me to dust myself off and

have an adventure again. You probably had no idea your friendship is exactly what the doctor ordered.

33

April 19-25, 2013

Days 204-210

How do you describe what it's like to let the current guide you gently under 60 feet of salt water, plankton, and rainbow-colored fish? How can I convey the feeling of looking up and seeing the surface of the waves from the underside? What words can be said to communicate the feeling I get when I see an octopus, gasp into my regulator, and swim back to beckon my diving buddies while clumsily making the hand gesture, using my fingers to mimic tentacles?

I've often said to non-divers who are thinking of taking the literal plunge that as a traveler, it's another frontier you get to see. It's another world to explore where all of the residents look different, speak another language, and subscribe to a different culture. Some are curious and swim circles around you as you descend into the blue; others are shy and it's a treat just to catch a quick glimpse of them.

Back in Melbourne, when I bought my ticket to return to Asia, I simultaneously booked this diving trip again. It gave me something to look forward to, and boy, did it deliver!

It was the final of my 18 dives over the course of 6 days on a live-aboard ship off the Andaman Coast when I finally saw a manta ray for the first time. We were about 20 minutes into the dive, and I started to worry I had seen all that I was going to see in this part of the sea. Then, a rapid series of taps made their way through the water and to my ears. This was a dive master out of my line of vision tapping on his air tank – a common way of saying, "something amazing is nearby!"

The divers in my group all spun around and looked at each other. Where was it coming from? Would we have a chance to see whatever this other group had seen? A few minutes later, a giant manta ray, spreading his wings like a majestic eagle, soared overhead.

I let the current carry me, I was so mesmerized. I was so blown away. It was like I was a lifelong birder who had finally seen a rare species that had previously been a mere rumor to me. Just as it was all sinking in, another one soared overhead, turned around, and came back my direction, bathing himself in the bubbles emitted from our regulators.

The rest of the dive is a blur to me. All I can remember now is the angelic glide of the ray, his sheer size, and the feeling of finally seeing one after searching for nearly a week. We surfaced a short while later, feeling gratified, satisfied, and elated by what we had seen. One of my dive buddies was still crying tears of joy.

Yes, it is a strange and difficult thing to convey the sheer amazingness of scuba diving.

34

April 25, 2013

Day 210

I turn 27 tomorrow, and birthdays are one of those times when you stop and reflect, aren't they? Truthfully, I don't know where I'm going or what I'm doing. I feel a little lost which I suppose is not surprising given my propensity to wander.

Sometimes I think to myself, "Man, I'm so cool. I wanted to do something and now I'm out there freakin' doing it! You only live once, baby! Live for the moment!" and more self-elevating fluff like that.

These moments of elation are usually followed shortly thereafter by thoughts of, "Seriously, what am I doing? My money is dwindling. Aren't I supposed to be engaged and popping out spawn by now?"

And then, "But I don't really want spawn..."

Followed by "Yes, yes you do!"

The mental battle is usually kind of like that.

On the road, long-term travelers are everywhere. What I did by quitting my job to travel is not that impressive, surprising, or novel. Sure, I'm trying to travel for as long as I can. Of course I'm going to go as long as my money allows me.

Naturally I'm trying to see as much of the world as possible. We're all in that boat. Move on, there's nothing special to see here.

It's when I talk to friends who are stateside, living the life that I used to, that I start to realize I've taken a path unlike any of theirs. I start to realize that they have direction, and I don't. They have a routine. It involves waking up at 7 AM, heading to work, breaking for lunch around noon, driving home, maybe heading to the gym, making dinner, watching TV, falling asleep, rinse, repeat. I did not value this when I lived it, but it's funny how the older I get, the less adult I feel because I don't have this routine anymore.

Because I'm supposed to by my late 20s, right?

People in the Western world say things like, "So, you just travel all of the time? Did you win the lottery or something?"

To which I say, "No, I write about Buddhist temples. I do cool things like ride motorbikes in between haggling over dollars and cents and trying not to look like a sweaty hot mess. Do you know how hard it is to look sexy with several layers of DEET, humidity, and sunscreen on? Very hard, my friend, very hard."

It's like Southeast Asia is my parallel universe where lying on the sand or an open-air bamboo hut opens my eyes to the reality that all I really need in life is food, shelter, and good people. Then I turn a year older and wonder if it's completely unrealistic to wander without establishing something more lasting.

What I keep coming back to, and what I'm trying to figure out is, is it possible to ever truly be happy? The grass is always greener somewhere I'm not, and that's why I've resigned myself to wandering until I find a green enough patch to rest my tired feet on for a while. But truth be told, the grass always browns, withers and dies right before my eyes. I suppose all I have to do is water it, but I never do.

Do you ever wonder, just a little bit, what it's all for?

I sure do.

35

April 26, 2013

Day 211

Remember when I left the Thai islands over New Year's because I was tired of the debauchery? Remember how I meditated instead of attending the full moon party because I just couldn't handle another wild, crazy party?

Remember how Joshua made me feel like garbage the day that I got my last monk tattoo? Well, screw all of that. I'm throwing all of that out and starting anew.

I turn 27 today and it just so happens to be the full moon party again on Koh Phangan, and I simply couldn't ignore that coincidental date. So here I am, sitting in a shared female dorm on the island I spent Christmas on with a bunch of awesome English girls. They'll be my partners in crime for the next few days. I love how easy it is to just walk into a hostel and make a bunch of new friends. Traveling has been a blessing that way.

A few days ago, I also got another Sak Yant tattoo in the middle of my upper back – the Gao Yord or nine-spire. It serves as another protective tattoo from black magic and bad luck. The nine spires represent the nine peaks of Mount Meru which is a legendary mountain from Buddhist and Hindu mythology that is thought to be the center of the universe. A little Buddha is etched onto every level of the nine spires and the lines reaching upwards are meant to lead me toward enlightenment.

It's my birthday gift to me, and there was nobody around this time to make me feel bad about it or like it was something I shouldn't do.

That was a few days ago, and tonight I'm going to dance. I'm painting myself with neon paint, taking nothing but some money and my key out with me, and I'm giving myself permission to be wild and free as all good things are.

Goodbye 26, you were transformational in so many ways. I'm thankful rather than fearful of another year and when I look back on everything, it's been nothing short of a privilege to make it this far in life in years, memories, and distance.

36

April 27, 2013

Day 212

Now *that* was a night!

It began with a few card games and drinks with the girls from my dorm, painting ourselves in neon paint and jumping on the back of a songthaew, which is a truck/taxi, holding on while standing on the back bumper as we drove through winding roads from one side of the island to the other.

Little stands lined the walkway into the venue, full of aggressive touts trying to sell anything from buckets full of alcohol to glowing headbands and shirts.

My new friends tried to buy me a bucket but I politely declined. I've seen them poured before and they consist of roughly four shots of alcohol and one can of Red Bull with amphetamines in it, because this is Thailand and here it's legal. I knew that would send me over the edge and I wasn't interested in getting that sloppy that night.

Another tout refused to let us through without buying an "entrance bracelet." We knew entrance was supposed to be free but the bracelet was cool and cost next to nothing so we bought it anyways, not keen to argue.

The party takes place on the beach and is full of stages

blasting techno music. Hours went by dancing and I have no idea where the time went, but somewhere in the middle of it all I lost the girls I entered with and ended up with a semi good-looking, and probably 22-year-old, British kid on my arm.

Throughout the night we jumped from platform to platform, dancing until the sun came up. As it rose, my surroundings were finally illuminated. For starters, I could finally see the debauchery around me. People practically had sex ankle-deep in the ocean and I felt bad for the locals. Their beach was overrun with badly behaved tourists, and I would hate us if I were them.

I wandered down to the water, boy toy in tow and marveled at the sunrise unfolding in front of me. Sharp, jagged rocks punctuated the calm sea as the sun started to peek over the horizon. This was easily one of the best sunrises I've ever seen.

I was transfixed, almost forgetting where I was or who I was with. I felt a tug on my arm that brought me back to reality.

"I have to go now, my ferry is leaving soon," he said.

"You can't go at a time like this!" I replied. "This is clearly the greatest sunrise anyone has ever seen, ever!"

"Come to Koh Phi Phi with me," he offered.

I stood for a moment on the shore, considering his proposal on one hand and unable to tear myself away from the magnificent sunrise on the other.

Remember how I'd been to Tonsai en route to Koh Phi Phi but elected not to check it out because I simply couldn't tear myself away from that beach? I'd missed out on experiencing Phi Phi in person, but if photos are any indication it does look amazing. That blue water and white sand was the inspiration for the book and movie *The Beach*. Besides, he was super cute.

"Have a good trip," I replied, "I'm staying here."

I'd made the mistake of following a guy before and I wasn't going to make it again. The rest of this trip was about one person only – me – and I had other plans.

A bit dejected, he nodded in understanding and slowly moved away, letting go of my hand. I gave him a smile and turned back toward the water, watching as the fiery red sun fought with the water until it was finally freed, rising up above the placid ocean, reflecting on the rocks, and painting everything a burning red in its wake.

"Welcome to 27," I said quietly to myself. "It's going to be a great year."

Part 7

Malaysia: The Land of Unexpected Adventures

37

April 30, 2013

Day 215

Upon my departure from Thailand after a combined three glorious months, the familiar mixture of unease and excitement that accompanies landing in a new country came over me. I knew almost nothing about Malaysia and wasn't sure what to expect after becoming so comfortable in Thailand.

Yesterday, apart from dinner, wasn't that exciting. In fact the last few days have just been a series of ferries and buses to get here, and today is the first day that I explored much of anything.

I've come to Georgetown in Penang, Malaysia, and immediately the most apparent difference between Thailand and Malaysia is the ethnic diversity of Malaysia. There's a little India here in Penang with cheap bracelets and bindis for sale everywhere. Last night I found a chicken curry samosa stand that sells freshly made samosas, folded up and fried on the spot, that cost less than 4 Ringgit ($1). As I walked down the street, away from Little India and back to my guesthouse, I thought to myself, "This is delicious, I can die happy now." I told a guy from my hostel where to find it and he came back and said the exact same thing.

Today I visited Kek Lok Si, a traditional Chinese temple rumored to be the largest Buddhist temple in Asia. I believe this is true because it towers over the neighborhood covering a plot of 30 acres and features over 10,000 Buddha statues inside. I also loved the blend of Chinese and Thai architecture styles in some of the pagodas which were tall enough to have three levels and provided a gorgeous view of Penang. The Chinese characters printed along many of the walls took me back to my time studying the language in Taiwan and I felt comforted.

What I loved about Kek Lok Si was the calm feeling. It's large enough to welcome plenty of visitors without feeling crowded and, thankfully, much less famous than the Grand Palace in Bangkok which I still shudder at when I think about how hot, frustrating, and sweaty that day was. In contrast, today was breezy and felt calm and spiritual – just what I needed.

I like Malaysia so far, and I can't wait to see what the next few weeks hold.

38

May 10, 2013

Day 225

I flew to Kuala Lumpur a few days ago, and it has been a whirlwind of roti canai, an Indian-inspired flatbread with a spicy lentil curry called dhal, and milo in a bag with a straw, which is basically chocolate milk. Malaysia has quickly worked its way to my heart through my stomach.

I received a message a few days ago from a local girl named Syaza, a raven-haired, petite beauty with near-perfect English and a noble presence. She has been following my Instagram account and asked if I'd like to meet in person. I feel pretty lucky to have had this opportunity fall into my lap, and I agreed without a second thought to have lunch with her.

Then she asked if I'd like to attend a traditional Malaysian engagement ceremony with her. At first I worried; is that weird? They don't even know me but I'm going to be a guest at such a big event? Then again, how could I pass up an opportunity like that? I said yes and today we went together. It was beautiful.

The day started at Syaza's place.

"Would you like to wear a traditional Malaysian outfit to the engagement ceremony?" she asked.

"Absolutely!" I excitedly replied. However I couldn't help but notice that I stand a full head taller and couldn't imagine anything she had would fit me.

She rummaged in her sister's closet and pulled out a deep blue silk Kabaya – a traditional outfit with long pants and a long-sleeved tunic shirt. This one was adorned in gold and silver beads and sequins. It was stunning.

"You look beautiful in that!" said her lovely mother as we prepared to leave the flat and head to the event.

A Majlis Tunang is an elaborate Malaysian engagement ceremony that involves the gift giving to the couple. The gifts are traditionally flowers and cakes given by a representative of the groom to a representative of the bride. This is the way in which he asks for her hand in marriage. Both sides use poetic language of love during the exchange.

I was told that typically this type of affair only involves women as guests, although in these modern and more progressive times men are more likely to attend the event as well.

We walked in to see that all of the furniture had been cleared – it is typical to sit on beautiful rugs on the floor. A red couch covered with flowers and soft pillows had been placed in the middle of the room. The gifts were arranged in front. It was all quite thoughtful and intricate.

This is just one of many ceremonies I came to understand as typical of a Malaysian marriage, which can sometimes involve two additional weeks of marriage ceremonies following the engagement, which is preceded by a pre-engagement. It's quite involved, but when I compare it to the American version that involves an engagement party, bridal shower, bachelorette party, rehearsal dinner, and finally a wedding, I realize we're not so different after all.

Following the ceremony, everyone ate a feast of Malaysian food.

I was warmly welcomed by the stunningly beautiful bride and her family and told to help myself to as much food as I wanted. They were concerned that it may be too spicy for me, but I grew up on spicy Mexican and Asian foods in Southern California and therefore had no problem happily stuffing my face with biryani rice, chicken, beef, and of course cakes.

When we finished with the meal, the bride-to-be's younger sister presented us with a gift of small cakes and a book of Islamic prayers. When we left, we shook both hands of each family member, touched our head to our hands, and then brought our hands to our hearts. Syaza's mother explained this to me as a way of showing respect. I hope I got it right. I was just copycatting everyone else's moves.

I felt incredibly welcomed by everyone there, and I felt very lucky to have had the opportunity to be a part of something that most tourists never get to see.

Many thanks to Syaza for inviting me. I can already tell that we'll be friends for life.

39

May 16, 2013

Day 231

After several days exploring Melaka and the outskirts of Kuala Lumpur with Syaza, who never let me pay for anything at all, always sneaking off to pay the bill before I even noticed, the time finally came for me to bid a sad goodbye and explore more of Malaysia.

I did some Google image searches and became entranced by the beauty of Cameron Highlands, a tea-growing region just a few hours' bus ride away. It's already apparent that Malaysia is a much richer country than any of the others I've visited in Southeast Asia so far. It's a bit more expensive, but it's definitely still a 'budget' destination.

Flash-forward to today: I've just come back from a gorgeous hike in a nice and cool setting, which is a new feeling for me in an otherwise hot and sweltering Southeast Asia.

The brisk mountain air greeted me, and I felt at ease. The last time I found myself in the mountains was in northern Thailand, way back at the beginning of December. I hadn't realized how much I missed them until today.

Cameron Highlands can be a bit touristy, but I've found a little nook away from all of the hotels. It's a small colonial chalet that opened just three months ago, and I'm the only guest.

I began today with jungle trek number one, through snarled tree branches and mud, narrowly avoiding low hanging branches and grabbing onto tree roots for support as I climbed hand over foot, wiping off the occasional spider web to the face during the steep climb. I was astounded that I emerged without a blanketing of mosquito bites despite not wearing DEET – it must have been a combination of the cool weather and altitude.

It has been months since I've felt comfortable outside. This time, I was sweating from pure hard work rather than a heat-induced suffering.

After two hours of climbing almost directly uphill, I looked around at the apex of the mountain and was rewarded with astounding beauty. I felt like I should yodel or something.

A familiar feeling crept over me and breathed life into me. I'm happy again, I'm grateful again, and I'm in the moment again, here in the Cameron Highlands.

When I passed by a strawberry farm, an enthusiastic fruit picker took photos of me playing the giant strawberry game – he held up the strawberries close to the camera while I stood back and put my hands around an imaginary giant strawberry, creating a humorous photo in the process. Then he helped me pick a few choice berries and squeezed fresh strawberry juice from them.

He explained that he's from Bangladesh and has been in Malaysia for about ten years but sends almost everything back home to his family. I tipped him extra for his efforts and continued on my way.

I think it must be some kind of unwritten rule: tea plantations can only exist in perfectly beautiful settings with misty rolling hills.

The road was mostly quiet, blessing me with a pleasant walk through the country roads. My terminus was the tea plantation where I watched a harvest take place in the distance and sipped on rose and lychee tea while eating scones. Something about it just felt so right, so peaceful, and so delicious.

It might be the extremely friendly locals, the change of scenery, or simply switching it up enough to shock my system a little, but I'm glad to have my travel mojo back again after feeling as though I might have lost it.

Before I turned in for the evening I finally felt like doing something I hadn't done since January – I meditated. It seems that a day spent hiking through the Cameron Highlands was just what I hadn't realized I really needed.

Now it's time for a bucket shower, mixing hot and cold water, and a nice long sleep.

40

May 17, 2013

Day 232

Today the owner of my guesthouse, Krish, asked if I'd like to come to a local party in the Cameron Highlands.

Throughout my travels, I have learned that when a local invites me to an event, the answer should always be "yes." When he added that the food was free and the draught Guinness was free-flowing, my commitment solidified.

It was a dinner and karaoke session hosted by the Cameron Highlands elite, and I was invited.

An hour or so before taking off, Krish informed me that since I'd be the only foreigner, there was no way I'd get out of performing karaoke on stage. I told Krish I can't sing to which he retorted with an evil chortle.

We arrived a short time later to a mixed crowd of Chinese-Malaysian and Indian-Malaysian attendees. Krish found it hilarious to introduce me to everyone as a singer from Hollywood, thereby cementing my fate.

The party started normally enough. We all filled our plates with delicious Indian food and socialized. Next, an informational video about a dietary supplement played for about twenty minutes, followed by a passionate and heartfelt weight loss story by an attendee. I could make out very little of what was said (as I'm not a Malay speaker) but found it odd that we had just eaten plates of fried food. Oh, and next we were having cake.

He finished by pointing to a pile of supplements and offering them for 20 Ringgit apiece. It was quite a unique opening to a party.

I thought that perhaps in the hype of the moment that everyone had forgotten that a (fake) singer from California was in the audience, but he finished his speech by thanking us, especially "our special guest from California, who would be singing later," for attending. I cringed.

A couple of songs went by sung by others – one a traditional Indian song and the other a love ballad in Chinese. Then, Krish mischievously took over the microphone and announced that I would be singing a song.

I hung my head, downed my glass of Guinness for some liquid courage, and walked over to the karaoke booth to make my choice. It was clear I was not getting out of this one.

Have I mentioned that I have never, ever sung in front of anyone? I mean, the shower walls and the inside of my car have certainly heard my singing voice, but even they were silently protesting, I'm sure of it.

My sincerest hopes that a Taylor Swift ballad would be available were dashed when the entire booklet appeared to be stuck in the '90s. Thankfully there was some Maroon 5 in there to save the day, er, night, as it were.

I greeted the crowd in Mandarin, picked up from my studies in Taiwan years ago, and apologized for my poor singing ability. This alone elicited cheers. I instantly felt better.

Missing most of the high notes but managing not to shatter any glass or make anyone in the audience cover their ears and beg through bitter tears for the terrible noise to stop, I finished the song and hoped I'd be done with it. I tried to run off stage.

But, no, they demanded an encore. This time, I sang "Killing Me Softly," as I can only manage deep-voiced songs, to music that was a bit off, and ran off stage insisting I was done singing.

"Singing makes you young," said Krish.

I think it just made me feel sober.

I spent the rest of the night going around the room saying, "Hen gaoxin renshi ni," (nice to meet you) over and over – the crowd was suddenly much more interested in this foreigner who could speak some Chinese – followed by dancing to a variety of '50s swing, hip-hop, and Bollywood songs.

I was not allowed to sit in my chair and resist dancing. Each time I tried, I was pulled back up.

It was my mastery of all of the moves to "Gangnam Style" that earned me the compliment, "You dance really well!" I had a hunch that one day I'd be glad I had learned the leg-kick-wrist-knock combo.

Somewhere between it all, I found myself laughing and enjoying the small party in the misty mountains of Malaysia more than I would have enjoyed a booming Hollywood nightclub. It was easily the most ridiculous night of my trip thus far.

And I mean that in the best possible way.

41

May 21, 2013

Day 236

Today I bonded with a puffer fish.

After the Cameron Highlands, I made my way over to Pulau Perhentian, an island off the coast of Peninsular Malaysia that is known for white-sand beaches and scuba diving.

It's a gorgeous island with just one budget hostel, and it fills up quite quickly. It's located in the jungly part of the island in between the two beaches so it's quite convenient to wander to the coral beach side during the day for diving and over to the sandy side at night for drinks under the stars and live reggae music.

The water is calm and shallow. You can see right through it to the yellowish-white sand, and I can understand why people love this little island so much. During the day it's an interesting juxtaposition as the local girls, wearing headscarves and long sleeves, swim in the water next to Westerners in bikinis. Nobody seems to mind each other, and as I've found in Malaysia, the friendly locals are happy to have guests in their country. Today wasn't a beach day for me, though. Today was a diving day.

The dives in Perhentian Island are pretty shallow which means the visibility is a bit better from the light shining through and the air lasts much longer. Plus I was able to dive without a wet suit which I always appreciate because squeezing into one of those isn't high on my list of favorite things to do.

Today we dove at a site called Sail Rock, and it was like a dream. The schools of fish constantly passing me by and the calm beauty all around me brought me right into the moment and like I belonged down there.

Then a bumphead parrotfish the size of my torso sailed by, giant, blue, and majestic. They're so named for the bulbous bump on the front of their heads which is apparently used for battling each other for dominance during the mating season.

After he passed, three puffer fish, larger than I'd ever seen before and about half the size of the parrotfish, came towards me for a closer look. They were covered in giraffe-like markings and stared at me with their big, saucer-like eyes.

I floated a bit closer, but they did not swim away. They did not aggressively get closer, either as clownfish do when you get too close to their anemones.

They just stopped and observed me and I them. The moment seemed frozen in time. We could have stayed there for ages. I felt like, in some strange way, we bonded. It was like they were telling me, "You're all right with me," and I communicated back, "You're all right with me, too."

Just like that, I felt like I was in the right place.

I know I've been glazing over the experience in Melbourne lately and making it seem like it didn't happen and as though the past doesn't exist. It's because I had to put it out of my mind. I didn't want to let Joshua or the pain of goodbye kill what was left of this trip. Today as I lie in the ocean after surfacing from the dive, I finally feel cleansed. The final remnants of him washed away. I spread my arms, and I finally felt free again.

The past is okay with me. Everything that brought me to this point is just fine. All of the things that felt so good and so horrible in the moment led me to this point, and it's all a learning experience anyways, isn't it?

Goodbye for good, Joshua. Goodbye forever.

42

May 28, 2013

Day 243

"If you want to try it, I know of a way to do it for cheap," he said to me from the dorm bed across the room.

I had only just met him, and we were talking about doing something fairly major together. I hadn't planned for it and, frankly, was ill prepared for what awaited me. Still, I was so intrigued – I told him that I'd like to try it.

We awoke early the next morning and set out on foot, casually talking about our past travels and avoiding focusing on the monumental task ahead of us: We would be climbing Mt. Kinabalu in Borneo, Southeast Asia's tallest mountain, in just one day.

I flew to Borneo after impulse buying an $18 ticket with Air Asia when I was on Pulau Perhentian. I knew signing up for the newsletter would prove to be a good idea! I landed here in Sabah, Borneo, without much of a plan other than another dive I'd booked in Sipadan in one week's time. I didn't have a clue of what else people do here.

Then I found out about Mt. Kinabalu. I also found out that it costs hundreds of dollars to climb it over the course of two days. I wrote it off because of the cost, but still wanted to visit the area it's located in. That's how I came to meet Ned, the guy I'd end up climbing with.

Most people train for this, plan ahead, and book several weeks or days prior. I, however, hyperventilate when I have to plan things far in advance, so I didn't do anything of the sort.

That's where Ned, a tall, sandy-blonde-haired and good-natured guy from England, came in. He had looked into it and discovered that for closer to $65 per person, one could climb the mountain in one day and avoid staying in Laban Rata, the lodge at the 6km mark that held a monopoly on the area, and therefore set the prices sky-high for an overnight stay and food.

The catch is, to reach the summit Mt. Kinabalu in one day, one must make it to the top by 1 PM, leaving only five and a half hours to make it to the peak at 4,095 meters (13,440 feet). This would seem entirely doable given it is only 8.7km (5.4 miles) to the top; however, given the elevation gain of 2,229 meters (7,313 feet) and the thin air, this is no easy task.

The hike was, to put it bluntly, brutal. There were no flat parts to speak of.

If it weren't for Ned, who graciously carried my camera, water, and food, and who also kept up a very positive attitude that lifted me as well, I doubt I would have made it to the top.

The beginning was only a light taste of what was to come. It was mainly stone steps punctuated by the occasional steep wooden staircase. Each half-kilometer seemed like a feat of mankind and leg strength. At about 15 minutes per half km, we were making decent time.

Around the 6th kilometer, I started to worry I might not make it. I sat down next to Ned, panting, as we took a peanut butter sandwich break. It was a bit tougher than we both had bargained for.

"I can't get this close and not make it to the summit," he said.

I realized that I couldn't, either.

The final 2.7 kilometers were the toughest. We gained 1,000 meters of elevation over that short period alone. It started to take me 25 minutes per half kilometer. I asked Ned to go ahead, just in case I didn't make it by 1 PM. I didn't want to hold him back. The guide stayed with me and Ned disappeared into the distance.

Just as I thought I might not be able to go any further, I remembered I had brought along my iPhone and plugged in my headphones. Why hadn't I thought of this sooner? Music always gets me through the tough parts.

Clouds of icy rain formed around me as I came to a part so steep that it was almost vertical. I gripped the rope and climbed ever higher, as quickly as my legs, lactic acid screaming through them, would allow me. About .7 km from the top, I started to feel dizzy from the altitude.

"Just a bit further! We can make it!" my guide smiled to me. I glanced at the time on my phone and realized it would barely be possible. I was going to do it. I was going to make Mt. Kinabalu my bitch.

Finally I glimpsed the summit. Ned was sitting there smiling – he had made it about 45 minutes earlier. As I climbed the final step, he held out his watch. It read 12:57pm. I had done it, just barely.

Finally, a feeling of elation came over me. I was on top of Borneo resting with the clouds at the summit. If you'd asked me the afternoon before, I would have had no idea I'd reach the summit of Southeast Asia's highest mountain. The serendipity of travel never ceases to amaze me.

We took in the vista for about 20 minutes before heading back down the mountain. Unfortunately for me, what goes up must come down. We had 8.7km of stone steps to take on and complete before 5 PM.

Ned and I each slipped and fell in the mud on the way down, cursing our jelly legs every so often. We made it down just as the sun was setting – closer to 6 PM. Then I realized that we still had a 2km walk back to the guesthouse in front of us. I whined to myself on the inside and faked a smile on the outside.

As we started down the road, a group of Singaporeans we'd met at the guesthouse the night before who had also attempted the mountain pulled over and opened up the trunk of the van and offered us a lift. I loved them so much in that moment. Four of them had attempted to summit but only one actually made it.

That night, we sat around the big round table in the dining room while a couple of Chinese tourists with gigantic cameras took about 1,000 photos of the moths gathering outside the lights on the deck and local children sat all around us asking questions like where we were from and how many siblings we had. What a day!

All in all, the climb was, of course, worth it. I proved a little something to myself and realized, through sore knees and walking like an 80-year-old down stairs for the past two days, that with a positive attitude and determination, almost anything is possible.

Now Ned and I are back in the capital of Kota Kinabalu and you'll never believe what we have planned next.

43

June 2-5, 2013

Days 248-251

"I was thinking to myself, this is crazy! I'm riding a motorbike through Borneo with two people I met only a few days ago!"

Ned had a valid point. We had only met a few days before, randomly, in a dorm before deciding to climb Mount Kinabalu together in one day. A few days before that, I had met Andrew, a muscled, brunette guy from Scotland in his early 20s who told me he planned to motorbike around Sabah, the northern state of Malaysian Borneo. The three of us ended up meeting by chance back in Kota Kinabalu and decided to take the trip together.

We were staying at one of the only guesthouses in town, and it turned out they had two motorbikes they were willing to rent to us. That was perfect because I'd only be going down to Semporna, the jumping-off point for my diving trip in Sipadan. I'd ride on the back of Andrew's bike and Ned would take the bags on the other.

Things started to go awry before we even took off. It seemed there was no real need to book a couple bikes ahead of time, so we didn't. When the morning came that we wanted to get going, of course, the bikes had been rented out. A few were getting fixed in the shop and would be back in the afternoon. We waited.

Finally the bikes arrived and we were off, albeit much later than planned – stopping once in search of rope as the bags were slipping out of place on the back of Ned's bike. Some friendly locals gave us some and we were on our way again.

Then the series of unfortunate events unfolded.

All seemed to be going well until, an hour out of Kota Kinabalu, the back tire of the bike Andrew and I were riding went flat. We were pretty much in the middle of nowhere at that point.

In contrast to Peninsular Malaysia, Malaysian Borneo is much more rural and the locals are less used to seeing foreigners than they are in, say, Kuala Lumpur. We were marooned in the middle of a country road bordered by a string of rice paddies.

Extremely luckily, there was a small convenience store a few meters away that happened to have a pump and spanners. Andrew took the good bike and rode 12km to the closest town in search of a new inner tube for the tire – without his wallet.

The shop owner's wife, a Malay woman adorned in a black dress and wearing a black-and-blue-flowered headscarf, sat and had a conversation with me while we waited.

"Sister," she said gently, "How well do you know these men?"

I answered her honestly. I told her I had just met them a few days ago and that I'd been traveling throughout Southeast Asia on my own for the better part of the last eight months. She was astonished at this. She expressed concern that we were motorbiking all the way through Sabah. "Very dangerous," she warned. I assured her that we knew what we were getting into.

We'd been informed that there weren't good medical facilities in the areas we'd be traveling through. Andrew had been told, "If you're going to crash a motorbike in those remote jungles, you're better of dying than going to a hospital."

Yet the past few months have drawn the fear and reasoning right out of me, and I'm not thirsty for anything but adventures. The old Kristin was terrified of motorbikes, but now I look at them as a way to access parts of the country that most people never see. They're a means to freedom, and I love the feeling of the wind on my skin in this sweltering heat.

An hour passed and I started to get a bit concerned. Finally, Andrew showed up with a truck following him. A pair of locals had lent him the money for the tube and followed him all the way back to the bikes. He gave them the money with a little extra for their trouble and they drove away smiling and waving. Another local fixed the tire for us, expecting no compensation in return.

I had encountered such friendliness and kindness amongst locals all over Malaysia, but still, we were blown away.

The rain came and went. The sunset in the sky was brilliant. The way it all reflected on the surrounding rice paddies and natural beauty was astounding. Just as it grew dark, we found ourselves 30km from the Tip of Borneo – our first stop.

As we turned onto the bumpy and rocky back road to the Tip, the tire popped again.

Ned went ahead with the good bike while Andrew and I stayed behind with the broken one. We waited for 20 minutes before Andrew decided to start pushing the bike and I carried the helmets. We knew it would all work out and casually admired the starry sky and spoke about life and traveling.

Thirty or so minutes later, a pickup truck arrived from the guesthouse at the Tip of Borneo to save Andrew's back. We all shared a room that night and fell asleep as soon as our faces hit the pillows.

The next day I wandered out to the sand in the early morning and saw the most beautiful beach I have encountered in Southeast Asia. I know I say that all the time, but this beach was simply incredible, deserted, and full of white sand and crystal-clear blue water. There were tiny pine trees separating the road from the sand and little purple flowers growing all along vines that covered the little sand dunes several meters from the beach. It was a small and secluded cove and the best part about it is nobody else was around. It was all mine and the boys'.

Most people think that the best beaches in Southeast Asia are in Thailand, and while they certainly are nice, I've never had a beach with sand this white and water this clear all to myself. I imagine if this was in Europe there would be fancy hotels lining the beach and people renting out umbrellas for €5 per day. There wouldn't be a free spot of sand to speak of, and there would be little cocktails with paper umbrellas for sale for far too much money.

The Tip of Borneo, however, is so far off the tourist trail, without any public transport running directly to here, that the beach was mine that day.

I headed back to the guesthouse to see that Ned and Andrew had already gotten to work replacing the tire, and I got to work taking pictures because that's what I do best in these kinds of situations. They washed off in the cool blue water and we got ready to head out for a long day of driving.

Before we left, the girls at the guesthouse bashfully asked if we could take a photo together. This had happened to me all over Malaysia so it didn't come as a surprise. I flashed a peace sign and stood awkwardly in my bikini as Ned took the cell phone photo for them. They smiled wide and bid us goodbye.

Next we changed out of our wet clothes, strapped on the bags, and prepared to take on the next 300km of the journey through palm plantations and general nothingness. Sabah was once mainly jungle that has, quite sadly, been slowly but surely replaced by palm oil plantations. The same is true for much of Peninsular Malaysia and Sumatra in Indonesia. It took away from what I bet was once a very scenic drive but we enjoyed the adventure regardless.

A couple of times we stopped for gas and food, filling up empty water bottles with extra petrol because the gas stations were intermittent at best. We were careful to hide what we were doing since we'd been told not to fill up water bottles previously when we were closer to Kota Kinabalu. It's a bit of a risk carrying petrol around that way, but it's also a risk to run out so we went with the lesser of two evils.

Our lunch break was certainly an interesting one. We drew a crowd of onlookers from the village as we tried to order food. There was a definite language barrier but I'd been in Malaysia for a month by then and knew the names of foods. I ordered us mee goreng ayam, fried noodles with chicken, and what came out was more or less what I'd envisioned, though I wished I had ordered a vegetarian dish as the chicken was more like jerky than meat. Andrew got up to stretch his legs and came back shaking his head.

"You definitely don't want to know what the kitchen looks like," he said grimly.

For the remainder of the drive, the roads were somewhat rough in places but we managed without breaking any limbs. That night, we stopped in a roadside hotel and ate Chinese food for dinner, downing a few beers – the first I'd had in over a week – and calling it another early night.

The next day we had another long drive through similar terrain, finally making it through without any popped tires or other fiascoes. The worst was that Ned ran out of gas only a half a kilometer outside of the coastal town of Sandakan and had to push the bike downhill towards town while Andrew and I went ahead to search out accommodation. All in all this seemed a small price to pay for what was an otherwise seamless journey.

Sandakan is a non-notable town that most tourists stop in so that they can see the orangutans in nearby Sepilok where there's a feeding platform. We stopped by but I was unimpressed, looking forward to the sightings that were rumored to be better in Sumatra. There were way too many tourists, and the experience seemed too fake. A ranger came and dumped out some fruit and vegetables and the orangutans slowly made their way over. One of them tipped over the bucket of water and another got down on the ground and slurped it up which was the highlight as it was pretty funny to see such humanlike movements.

I'd bought another cheap Air Asia flight to Medan, the capital of Sumatra, back when we were in Kota Kinabalu and silently hoped it would be better than this manufactured experience.

Today I parted ways with the boys. They're heading back up to Kota Kinabalu and I'm taking a bus down south to dive off the coast in Sipadan. I hugged each and sadly said my goodbyes. I know chances are good that I won't see either one again.

I'm so thankful for the opportunity to have had this adventure in Borneo. Nearly everything has been spontaneous and wonderful, and I owe it all to the fact that I'm traveling on my own, able to follow these whims. Through flat tires, rice paddies, beautiful sunsets, skies full of stars, rainstorms, random acts of kindness, and filthy clothes, it's something I'll always be glad I did.

Andrew and Ned, I'm left with the same quote running through my head, said by my favorite, A.A. Milne in *Winnie the Pooh*:

> "As soon as I saw you I knew an adventure was going to happen."

44

June 6-9, 2013

Days 252-255

Diving in Sipadan has been wonderful. I thought that the diving was good in Thailand and Pulau Perhentian, but it had nothing on the incredible underwater menagerie of Sipadan.

This spot is perfect for both the big and the small things, and I'm a huge fan of both. I love testing my buoyancy abilities by getting within inches of the reef and scanning for little nudibranchs, which are incredibly bright, neon-colored little sea slugs that look like they have tail feathers. They're not as easy to spot as they're usually about half the size of your pinky finger, but they can get as big as two thumbs pressed together.

The big stuff in Sipadan is mind-blowing. There are schools of barracuda so huge that it looks like a cloud of large swimming shields of silver. They part in plumes as divers swim through. Instead of the single bumphead parrotfish I saw in Perhentian, I saw a whole school here. There were black and white-tipped reef sharks all around which are always a joy to see. I just couldn't believe the density of the creatures here, and I worry I've spoiled myself to the point that any dive after this will pale in comparison.

Above water, the sights are equally amazing. I'm staying

on Mabul Island since nobody is allowed to overnight on Sipadan, and the dive center shares it with local Bajau people known colloquially as sea nomads or sea gypsies.

They really do live their lives on the water, eating, cooking, and sleeping on long and narrow wooden boats. They're born, live, and die at sea. They can even hold their breath for several minutes underwater for spearfishing!

There's a sad side to their story, though. Most of them are stateless and don't have citizenship that allows them to work in Malaysia. They're incredibly poor, and those who live in Thailand have been largely grounded since the tsunami, forced to abandon the only way of life they know.

Most of the interaction with the Bajau here on Mabul is limited to glances from the dock that separates the dive center's area and theirs. The kids occasionally come by looking for empty bottles to return for a few cents and a soda if you'll spare it. I don't, though, because the sugar rots their teeth and I'm guessing they don't have access to dental care.

The symbolism of this dock as a barrier isn't lost on me. It's a wall between the haves and have nots of the world who are given this status simply by being born. I appreciate the privilege I have while simultaneously feeling incredibly guilty for it, then feeling guilty for the self-indulgent guilt, unsure of what I can do about it. Apart from spending my money locally, I'm still not sure how best to help. I don't have any real skills to put to use as a volunteer, and I'm not so arrogant that I think I know what these people need. I think they just need a place to live as they please, and I hope that's what this is for them.

The sun is setting on my final day in Mabul after nine

fantastic dives and I'm so glad that I made it out here. I'd randomly heard about it when I first arrived in Georgetown over one month ago and was told I had to book way ahead for the diving here. I couldn't have imagined that all of the adventures would lead me up to this point, and it seemed that everything happened just the way that it was meant to in order to get me here.

Today I found a letter underneath my pillow from Jack, a tall, blonde-haired and blue-eyed guy from Leeds who I've spent the majority of my above-water time with while on Mabul. He left a day before me since the beds in the dorm were all booked out tonight but says he'll be waiting for me on the dock when I come back to the mainland. We'll see if he keeps his promise.

45

June 12, 2013

Day 258

I spent the past few days on Labuan, a small island off of Borneo, with Jack. We didn't do a whole lot save for taking some walks and generally just hanging out. It was kind of nice to just relax for a bit after my otherwise quite active adventures in Borneo.

I'm waiting to board my flight to Sumatra now, and as the minutes tick by on my final moments of my six weeks in Malaysia, I have a few words I never said to him. So here's my open letter to Jack that he may or may not ever see:

I say goodbye again and I wonder why I've put myself through this yet another time. We embrace and part ways. You wish me well and look on from the taxi until he's driven you out of sight. I turn and walk into the airport; it's nearly time to board my flight.

I smile at the memories over the past week spent on beaches laughing in the waves and talking about what we saw under the water diving that day. I try not to think about the fact that I most likely won't ever see you again.

They say everything happens for a reason and that people come in and out of your life for some specific purpose. You repeated this to me the last night I saw you as I vigorously shook my head in disagreement. But I see what purpose you served now. I can see what purpose every ending serves. I learned something:

This is a mistake I will make again.

Before, there was Australia. It always goes the same way when I am asked where I have traveled this year. I give my chronological list and am met with confusion.

"That's a little out of the way, isn't it? Going to Australia and then coming back to Asia?"

Then I feel compelled to explain that I went there for a guy – for the pursuit of love, for the possibility of something that I thought was real. The same familiar, knowing expression crosses the face of the person across from me.

"Ah, made that mistake, did you? We've all been there."

I didn't see it then after the broken heart and the initial difficulty letting go, but I learned something from that experience too: if it was a mistake, then it is a mistake I will make again, and again.

Most long-term travelers run into this problem. We meet amazing new people constantly whom we inevitably have to say goodbye to. Relationships are tested and shortened on the road, whether they're friendly or romantic. Either way, people are constantly coming and going as if through a revolving door.

Some travelers have sworn off any type of scenario that involves the heart, unwilling to deal with the pain of goodbye. I guess I'm not there yet.

I know I'm setting myself up for hurt, but I can't help it. It'll happen again, and I'll groan when I see yet another couple's travel blog pop up. I will roll my eyes when I hear stories of other travelers meeting in paradise, selling off everything they own, and taking on the world together, and I'll feel a pain in my heart as I throw a book across the room when I get halfway through and realize it's going to turn into a love story.

The last thing I want to hear right now is a love song. It's to the point that if I see one more blog post about meeting Mr. Right on the road or another set of photos of a traveling couple, I might be sick.

Yet when the time comes again, and when the person is right again, I know I'll move across the world, take on a new adventure, or change my trajectory completely, if that's what I have to do to make it work. I will make that mistake again, knowing that one day, it won't end up being a mistake at all.

I always have an open heart, and it makes me both a lover and a habitual hurter. It's the name of the game we travelers play, and I don't know how to play it any other way, mistakes and all.

Part 8

Indonesia: The Land of Beautiful Souls

46

June 15, 2013

Day 261

Hello Sumatra, land of coffee, orangutans, and apparently motorbike crashes.

Lake Toba is stop number one for many people when visiting Sumatra. I'd heard good things so I wanted to check it out for myself. A volcanic lake stretching for miles, Lake Toba is the perfect place to chill out, get into some local culture, crash a motorbike, and perhaps rescue some kittens.

I met up with a travel blogging couple, Mark and Lauren, a strikingly good-looking pair from Montréal, during this leg of my trip. Like many other bloggers I knew them electronically, and since we ended up in the same place at the same time, it seemed like the perfect time to finally meet in real life.

We took a couple of motorbikes out today with the intention of heading to a lake within Lake Toba which apparently has an island in the middle of it. That makes it an island, within a lake, within an island, within a lake, within another island, if that makes any sense at all. Apparently it's the only one in the world, so we wanted to see it.

Lauren rode on the back of Mark's bike and I drove my own.

It was pink with neon green butterflies on it. I took it as a good omen.

First we stopped at a Batak village. The Batak people, who claim that they used to be cannibals, originally settled Lake Toba before the days of tourists and motorbikes. They're not just any cannibals, though, as they used to eat people raw. Yes, raw! This treatment was reserved for the most evil criminals who were tried at what has now become a tourist hot spot — the stone chairs — and then executed in front of a crowd of townspeople who would later feast on the raw remains.

People in other towns around northern Sumatra will roll their eyes and say this is just a fable that the older generation tells the younger boys, but I like to believe it's true. It's just too creepy and amazing not to be!

German missionaries eventually converted the Batak people to Christianity through offering educational opportunities and earning the Batak people's respect by learning the local language. Therefore the practice of cannibal sushi has since died off. True or not, it was a fun history lesson.

After visiting the Batak village, we set our sights on the lake within the lake.

"The roads are very bad once you head off the main one," warned the guesthouse owner. I had heard that before, and it had fallen on deaf ears then just like it would again today. Unfortunately for me, she turned out to be extremely right.

The vistas from the steep drive made the journey worthwhile. The lake within the lake, however, was not all that impressive. I suppose this is a classic example of the quote, "It's the journey, not the destination."

The road, made treacherous by the giant rocks and sand, was fine going up but not so much coming down. Before I knew it, my brakes forced my back wheel to catch on a rock (or sand? Who knows) and spin out of control, causing the bike to fall to the left while I managed to jump off and flail to the right, somehow landing on my feet without so much as a scratch or bruise.

Mark heard the noise and came screeching to a halt. A look of shock went across his face. He fully expected to turn around and see carnage but instead saw me calmly standing next to the bike and planted firmly on my feet.

"How in the hell?" he asked as he came over, pushed the bike back up, and restarted it for me.

"Are you okay to get back on?" he asked.

"I don't think I have much choice!" I replied as I swung a leg over and hopped back on. Luckily most of the steep and rocky part of our journey was behind us.

We pulled back into the guesthouse to return the bikes. Luckily my bike already had scratch marks prior to my blunder, presumably from someone else making the exact same mistake, so returning it and saying, "Nope! No problems with the bike!" didn't end up being an issue. I'm counting my blessings considering how many of my backpacker friends have motorbike crash stories and the scars to prove it.

Genius that I am, I left my camera in the storage compartment under the seat of the motorbike when I returned it. The owner had already driven away with it, so Mark saved the day by going to fetch it and, on his way back, he noticed some orphaned kittens running across the road.

He searched for the mother but found nothing. The local

with him pointed to the trash can nearby and said they had climbed out. Someone had clearly dumped them in there.

Trying to serve as savior to three adorable two-week-old kittens, Mark asked a guesthouse owner whom we knew to have a small farm and some animals if he could take them in. He said that he could, but only on the condition that we book three nights of accommodation with him. Mark had some choice words for him.

He looked around a bit more but found nobody who was willing to take the cats, so Lauren announced, "We're taking them to Bukit Lawang!" knowing that the kind-hearted locals there would surely take them in.

The kittens were still suckling, so we emptied out an eye drop bottle and fed them every now and then with milk. I'd been ignoring my horrendous cat allergy and playing with them anyway, sneezing and wheezing as a result.

Tomorrow, the kittens safely packed in a backpack, we'll take the ferry, then an 8-hour car ride to Bukit Lawang, the jungle town in Northern Sumatra that Mark and Lauren have spoken so highly of.

47

June 19-27, 2013

Days 265 – 273

Mark and Lauren were right about Bukit Lawang. It's the perfect little jungle town and I'm unable to leave.

"Hi, Kristin! Where you go?" kind voices call out periodically as I walk down the dirt and rock path through the trees each day. Smiling faces greet me each time I turn my head to see who's calling. Somehow they've all memorized my name, and they knew it after my second day here.

"Come back in a few weeks, months, or years, and they'll still remember you," said Joanie, a tall and dark-haired Canadian girl who has made this adorable place her home for the next year. She loves the hospitality, too.

Bukit Lawang is a tiny orangutan trekking town in the north of Sumatra. It consists of one long, mostly dirt, road bordered by guesthouses and a little market. The locals live on the other side of the road in little huts but everyone swims in the same river that runs through town together. The jungle stretches on for miles on either side of the river, and sometimes you can spy an orangutan or some other primate from the banks. I'm staying across the bridge from this long dirt track at the only fully locally owned guesthouse in the area, Bukit Lawang Indah, which means beautiful Bukit Lawang.

Most tourists just breeze through, using it as a hub for the nights before and after their jungle trek, but I was told that there is good reason to stay longer – that there is more to the place than meets the eye. Days later as I write this, I realize how true that is.

Each time I meet someone new in Bukit Lawang, I tell him my name and where I am from. He'll usually sing a line from the song "Hotel California," and if I tell him any extra information, he'll be able to recount it as I walk by. Days later, he can repeat the same things right back to me without missing one detail.

I also loved the orangutan trekking here. It was everything I wanted it to be – more wild and through a real jungle than what was available in Sepilok back in Borneo. Robet, a local who grew up here, took me on a walk all on my own without any other tourists for only €25 and was the best guide ever. I can't believe what a bargain I got. He bonded with Manny and Olivia the last time they were here, and when they brought me back with them, they promptly introduced me and announced that Robet was the best guide in Bukit Lawang.

I believe it. Some of the other guides feed the orangutans to lure them closer, but Robet firmly condemns this practice and instead tracks them by smell. He was excellent at finding them well before the other tourists saw, giving me a chance to view them without any interruptions or competition for my viewing spot. I noticed the other guides would look for Robet because they knew if they found him, they'd also find orangutans.

There's very little about this town I don't like. There's no Wi-Fi which is kind of wonderful. I'm reading so many books and just enjoying the lazy days. Plus I have a vested interest in sticking around – there's the bundle of kittens we had rescued from Lake Toba and I need to be sure that they're happy and healthy. These days they get love from the whole community. Josie kindly took them in and they have been happy little trekkers ever since.

I spend my days going to Landah River with locals to avoid the Sunday karaoke (oh how it makes my head hurt), being asked to take pictures with the kids who pour in from neighboring Medan, renting inner tubes for 10,000 Rupiah (USD $1) and tubing down the river through town, jumping off of rocks into the water with local kids, picking the tube back up and hiking it to the starting point, and tubing right back down again.

What I love even more are the musical nights at my guesthouse. The guys who work here take out a guitar, bongo drums, and eventually a Bintang beer bottle and pocketknife, which becomes another instrument, nearly every night of the week. They belt out lyrics to popular songs, encouraging everyone in the room to sit in a circle and sing along.

They replace various lyrics with trekking terms:

> "You know you look so good (look so good), you
> know you look so fine (look so fine) you know
> you look se-xy (not really), you know you look
> just like an orang-u-tan in Bukit Lawaaang a
> bamba..." ("La Bamba")

"Would you know my name if I saw you in jungle? Would it be the same if I saw you in jungle?" ("Tears in Heaven")

"Welcome to the hotel Bukit Lawang. Such a lovely place, such a lovely face." ("Hotel California")

Some nights we go through so many bottles of beer that the side-by-side lineup of bottles spans several tables. This is for a whole room of people, though, I promise.

I never fear I'll get scammed here – something I've dealt with heavily in other areas of Southeast Asia. That's a good feeling. It's also been the cheapest week of my travels for a while now and one of my best fed. The day I downed an entire kilo of passion fruit in only 12 hours is still legendary. I can't understand why I'm the only one who thinks that's a good idea. Passion fruit is the definitive best fruit in the world, after all.

I'll find warmth in the memories of my weeklong stay here for years to come, I'm sure of it. Bukit Lawang, you're an unexpected hit and I have a feeling I'll come back to you one day.

48

June 28, 2013

Day 274

There's a little something here in Indonesia that's quite different from all of the places I've been so far in Southeast Asia. I started to really notice it over the past couple of days, and especially the other night, in Bukit Lawang.

A kid named Tiko sat right in front of me parked so close that there could be no misunderstanding. He was fabulous at the guitar and a phenomenal singer to boot. He belted out love songs, strategically replacing certain words with "Kristin" just in case there was any shadow of doubt that he was singing just for me. If not for the myriad Bintang beers the group had downed this might have been quite awkward, but everyone was laughing and singing along oblivious to the serenade, just as we had all night.

"What's going on here?" I wondered. "The men in the rest of Southeast Asia have avoided me like the plague, yet this guy is serenading me as if I'm the only girl in the room."

Seeing that his territory was in danger of encroachment, another hostel employee, Joru, asked me to step closer to the river and have a talk with him. We had spent that day escaping the Sunday karaoke by visiting a secluded river elsewhere in the jungle and napping in a tiny open-air tree house above the water. To me, it had been friendly. How silly that assumption had been.

"I really like you," he said. Perplexed, as I had honestly napped most of the day while he was off swimming, I asked how he could possibly like someone he barely knew.

"I like Western girls," he replied. I told him it was time to go back to the song circle and shortly thereafter called it a night, heading back, solo, to my room.

Then there was the guy who gave me a lift on his motorbike earlier in the week. He followed me back to the other side of the river today saying he wanted to go "swimming." What was lost in translation is he really meant "shower" in my room. What?

It took a few days in Sumatra to dawn on me that I was seeing the local boys constantly flirting with the Western girls – a phenomenon that was the exact opposite of what I had been seeing in Thailand where Western men were almost always with younger, much more beautiful, women.

The longer I stayed in Bukit Lawang, the more I learned. A couple consisting of a Western woman and Indonesian man own nearly every guesthouse in the area. Many girls come to visit who, it turns out, are girlfriends of the local guys. At first I didn't understand the fascination. There are so many things working against these couples: distance, cultural differences, not to mention a huge language barrier. Sure, many of them know all the words to popular Western songs, but sitting down and having a conversation is often rather difficult.

Last night I decided to observe with new eyes, watching the guys work their magic on girls they had taken trekking that day. I have to admit, there's something about the way they laugh freely and just enjoy life's simple pleasures that's refreshing. What's more, they give more undivided attention to these girls than they may ever get back home.

Trying to wrap my head around it, I talked to Joanie about all of the odd things that had been happening. She laughed knowingly and recommended a documentary to me that would help explain things: *Kuta Cowboys in Paradise*. The documentary followed what can only be described as gigolos in Kuta, Bali, who seek out Western women whom they believe may have money. They woo them, sometimes get into relationships with them, and develop a bond. Though money isn't directly exchanged for sex, they become kept men.

It seemed no different to me than some relationships between Thai women and Western men. The Westerners often support these guys financially, buying all of the food and paying for lodging while in Indonesia, then sending money over every now and then after returning home. It's so cheap for these women to buy a meal, a T-shirt, or pay for the room for the week, why not foot the bill in exchange for a good lover? What they don't know is they are often one of many girlfriends, and fidelity is not a given.

Some of my favorite quotes from the documentary were, "I score within three days. If not, don't stand by me. Many girls on the beach." Or, "What's important is the money's good. Not the face."

The best part was the guy who was willing to explain the process: First, he showers the girl with attention, then he takes her out and shows her a good time. It's key to be non-aggressive, always smile, and appear to care.

The most shocking part of all to me was that some of these men are married. I had read the same about Thai prostitutes in a fairly riveting memoir. It's insane to think about, but the wives are usually fully aware of what their husbands are doing. They need the money so badly, they put up with it. To make the pressure even stronger, these guys have an important role giving back to their communities as well.

Of course, not every relationship is based on this and like every documentary, this one is incredibly slanted towards telling the story of the guys who do this for financial gain. I'm sure that plenty of the relationships I saw were real and they truly loved each other.

I can't help but think back to an American guy I was chatting with in Thailand, asking him, "Don't you resent being used just for your money?" to which he replied, "No, it's mutual using, so who cares?" I suppose it's the same in Indonesia.

49

June 29 - July 5, 2013

Days 275-281

From Bukit Lawang, I soared over Indonesia by plane blowing the biggest chunk of my budget that I've blown yet on the most expensive domestic flight in, I don't know, ever? Perhaps I'm exaggerating but at just shy of $400 for a flight of a couple hours, it hurt. It was worth it, though, because I made it to Flores, the jumping-off point for Komodo National Park here in Indonesia.

I rushed over because I would be joining a six-day live-aboard diving boat to really test my diving abilities in some of the strongest current in Southeast Asia. Komodo is also supposed to have some of the best diving around including the very real possibility of seeing manta rays. I figured that if I did see them, it would be worth the money for sure.

My extravagant purchase was quickly justified when, during my first day of diving, a manta ray came so close to me that I thought it just might touch me. That is not an experience that I will soon, or probably ever, forget. A creature as huge and magnificent as a manta ray flying overhead then coming in closely and blessing me with her presence is a memory from this trip that I will always hold near and dear to my heart.

If you thought the following 20-odd dives would pale in comparison, worry not. I still can't decide which of the two spots is better between Sipadan in Borneo and Komodo in Indonesia. It's a toss-up because the corals are incredible in Indonesia. They're so colorful, varied, and plentiful. There were nudibranchs everywhere which I've come to really love seeing.

I saw all the usual suspects – moray eels, tons of sea turtles, parrotfish galore, reef sharks, and all kinds of other colorful reef fish – and a few less common guys such as seahorses and stingrays.

I've come to find that live-aboard dive boats are all more or less on the same type of schedule. Everyone wakes up pretty early, around 6 AM or so, for the first dive of the day. Next is a big breakfast followed by a break and another late morning dive. Then we usually lie in the sun on the top deck or take a nap on one of the benches in the shade until the afternoon dive, followed by more food, snacks in between, and a few card games and guitar songs at night unless there's a night dive which there was twice during the trip.

The time spent out of the water was beautiful, too. Komodo National Park is gorgeous. There are plenty of huge islands with long swaying grasses and the water is like a sapphire shade of dark blue. The sunsets were golden, then purple, and then the night sky was the most dazzling of all. Unobstructed by light pollution, the Milky Way was bright and beautiful.

Leah, a blonde, freckled, spunky American girl who was also a solo traveler, was paired with me for all of the dives. We had both been diving so much lately that our air consumption was low, which is a sign of a more advanced diver, and our buoyancy was on point. We eventually got assigned our own dive master for just the two of us, and on the final night we had one of the most spectacular dives I've ever had.

I considered skipping the dive altogether. It was at the end of the six-day trip and the night dives were problematic because there were only two showers on board. This meant the very real possibility of waiting, cold, for a turn in the shower. However I decided that it was silly to waste the money I'd spent on the dives just for a hot shower, so I took that final dive and I'm so glad that I did.

A Mandarin fish isn't something that commonly shows up in Komodo National Park. They're the size of a golf ball and covered in bright neon blue and orange splotches with little translucent orange fins that flutter in the water making them look like little birds. I didn't expect to see one at all until Leah waved her hand at me and beckoned me over. We were only in about 5 meters of water and there they were – two beautiful little Mandarin fish.

Now non-divers might wonder why this is such a big deal, but it's so incredibly rare to see these guys, especially at that time of day. Moreover, to have the view of them to yourself is also almost unheard of. There's a popular spot in the Philippines where you can find them but it's always chock-full of tourists. This was a real treat for us, the only two divers left in the water since we were so good with our air consumption.

I shook my dive master's hand under water as a 'thank you' for sticking with us for such a long dive, and we just floated there, spellbound. After 65 minutes we made the collective decision to surface and once we did, we were greeted by a sky full of dazzling stars. I looked over at Leah and wished her a happy Fourth of July. We had the best kind of fireworks imaginable glittering right above us in the form of constellations that night.

The final day of the trip, because you can't visit the park without trying to see Komodo dragons, we headed to Rinca Island.

"I don't think diving with Komodo dragons is really a good idea. They swim pretty fast, you know," said Pia, my dive master, when she saw my dismay that we weren't going to be diving with the Komodo dragons.

To be fair, I didn't realize how fast these guys could swim. I didn't know that nobody swims with them because they are dragons and their saliva is venomous, duh.

When we first arrived to the island, a ranger pointed us in the direction of the check-in where we began our walk around one of the island trails.

"Take a stick," he said to Pia.

She reluctantly grabbed one, her facial expression communicating exactly what I was thinking – what's a stick going to do against a dragon? However this seems to be the tool of choice for fending off bloodthirsty Komodo dragons, should we end up encountering one.

Moments later, we spotted the first few dragons. One was a baby and the others were full-grown adults. A few lumbered around in the shade and others were as lazy as could be in the sun. I guess I expected them to be ferocious, but in reality they were soaking up the sun like any other cold-blooded creature does when the sun is out.

There was one near the hut who had broken his legs during a fight with another dragon during mating season the previous year so he was a bit less dangerous to get close to for a photo. I crouched down and a ranger inched a bit closer to me, stick in hand just in case.

I honestly expected a much different experience with the dragons. I thought they'd be bloodthirsty reptiles of doom, but in reality they were a bunch of lazy bums. Just goes to show, once again I suppose, that traveling makes you realize how wrong your perceptions were all along and that maybe those animal shows on TV embellish from time to time.

50

July 6, 2013

Day 282

As I finished up my last dives I asked around for some intel for my journey from Flores to Lombok. Most tourists fly over or take a tourist boat to the tune of $200, but given their terrible sinking records in this strong current and the fact that I shelled out so much for my flight and the dive boat, none of that was in the cards for me.

I figured the locals must have some method of getting around, so that's how I would get around, too.

"What time does the boat leave for Sape in the morning?" I must have asked about five different people. I was told everything from 6 AM to 9 AM, so safe to say, it varies. I was advised that since I'm a "whitey" it would be best to show up early. Arriving at 7:30 AM, I decided this was true as I took one of the last seats available which was thankfully near a window.

Unlike tourist boats, the ferry is huge, transporting cargo and vehicles as well. I was much less worried about that behemoth sinking than a flimsy little boat in the strong currents of Indonesia.

The cost of the ticket was posted at 53,000 rupiah, which

is just over $5. I bypassed the man selling a combo ticket all the way to Mataram, the capital of Lombok, having heard that sometimes connections don't match up due to delays and the buses don't wait, making people lose out on the bus portion of the ticket. I'm not even sure what he would have charged, but if experience is any indication, it would have been more than I needed to pay.

Immediately, the old lady next to me with copper skin that was full of wrinkles, teeth that were stained with coffee, and hair that was covered in a pink floral scarf started speaking to me in Bahasa, holding out her hand and stroking my hair. She wanted money from me. I groaned and simply shook my head and looked out the window, the other direction from her. It had potential to be one long boat ride.

Around 9:45 the boat grumbled and started to move. I looked around. I was the only foreigner aboard. I thought to myself, "I've done it right."

It was packed to the brim with families taking over floor space sleeping, eating, smoking cigarettes, and chatting. Indonesia is the only country I've been to so far where cigarettes are openly advertised and smoked everywhere. I haven't met one man here who doesn't smoke cloves like a chimney. It doesn't matter how poor they are; the majority seem to buy cigarettes and chain smoke.

A poorly-made horror movie played in the background. I was glad to have brought along a good book and some music to listen to.

Over time the discomfort between the woman and I evaporated and I offered her cookies. She responded by offering me noodles and rice a couple of hours later. I offered her some peanuts; she insisted I take some bread and bananas. I bought us coffee. We became friends.

Before long, she gestured towards my sunglasses, indicating that she wanted to try them on. Then she and nearly everyone sitting around us was trying on my sunglasses and taking photos with me. I must be in, like, 100 random Malaysian and Indonesian people's Facebook photos at this point. We had somehow gone from an awkward situation to a downright hilarious and friendly one.

Communication was nearly impossible, but her daughter helped explain that they would help me get to Bima, the jumping off point for the next leg of my journey, and that the boy in the row ahead of us "liked" me, which I pretended not to understand.

The ferry docked six hours after taking off. Several public mini buses waited at the port to take us from Sape to Bima where I would then board a bus, then another ferry, and then board the bus once again bound for Mataram on Lombok.

Sure enough, the old lady motioned for a young man whose English was fairly decent to usher me to the same minibus as she was taking. He teased the others on the boat, "Why his English no good? He not finish school!" and then translated for me when another passenger said, "Lombok has a lot of coconuts," which they all found hilarious. I smiled awkwardly.

The bus took two hours and cost 25,000 rupiah, which is $2.50. I was sure to watch as the locals paid the same amount. We drove through truly stunning countryside of mainly rice paddies and palm trees. The bus stopped at a depot where I was immediately pointed out as the only foreigner as a swarm of ticket touts closed in on me. The posted price for the combo ticket for an overnight bus and ferry to Mataram was 210,000, but eventually, I bargained it down to 150,000 ($15).

The trip was long but relatively painless and worked like clockwork from there. The coach was nice enough although the chairs barely reclined and, per usual, my long legs hardly fit between my seat and the seat in front of me. After almost ten months in Southeast Asia, this is standard and does not bother me much anymore. Indonesian karaoke music blared in the background into the wee hours of the morning.

Finally, I arrived at the Mataram bus station around 7 AM, almost exactly 24 hours after I had started my journey in Labuan Bajo, Flores. My next stop was Kuta in Lombok which is nothing like the super seedy and touristy Lombok in Bali. This wasn't as straightforward as most of the busses weren't leaving for a few hours and the touts all conspired to charge me about the same for the trip as I'd paid for the entire previous 24 hours of transport. I finally found a motorbike, known locally as an ojek, driver to take me the two hours to Kuta for 90,000 rupiah and we were on our way.

All-in, it cost me 313,000 rupiah ($31.30), and once I reached my guesthouse, I basically collapsed on the bed and didn't wake up until nearly 14 hours later. Yet somehow I hold this memory dear and I'm so, so very glad that I did this instead of a two-hour flight. Traveling to the other end of the world was meant to be about these experiences.

51

July 8, 2013

Day 284

Kuta isn't my kind of place. It's a laid-back beach town, and I'm sure I would find it to be pretty if I walked around more, but it's mainly couples and I'm just not interested in fraternizing with such folk at this point. Nothing against the lovebirds, but they make me sick right now. Joshua is out of sight and mind, but I don't need any little reminders that I failed at a relationship already.

I chatted with Jack this morning. Remember the guy from Borneo? We still talk a bit, but ever since he told me he met up with another girl from long ago in his travels in Sri Lanka right after we parted ways and that he'd planned that long before even met me, I decided he can take a long walk off a short bridge. He wanted to have his cake and eat it, too.

In an effort to smooth things over and talk about absolutely anything else, he asked if I planned on climbing Mt. Rinjani while on Lombok. I didn't even know that's what people do here but yes, of course I plan to. I pretended like it was in my plans all along.

Like most things in Southeast Asia, the pricing online is pretty outrageous for pre-booking a Mt. Rinjani trek. I didn't have to wait long until the opportunity came to me, though, when a friend of my guesthouse owner came and made me an offer for a 3-day, 2-night trekking package with transport, food, guides, and porters. It was about a third of the price I found online and, after haggling, we settled on the equivalent of $100, which fit right into my sweet spot of roughly $30 per day (give or take a bit).

Early tomorrow, I'll head out to Senaru for a night and then I'll begin my trek. I've had an active past couple of months and I'm happy to continue the trend.

52

July 9-11, 2013

Days 285-287

I got on the bus yesterday bound for Senaru, and after speaking to a few of the people in there with me, realized that they charged everyone in my group a different price. It turned out I'd paid the least and was glad that I haggled a bit. My time in Southeast Asia has taught me well.

I settled into the basic guesthouse in the misty hills and awoke early the next morning to start the hike. I had a fantastic group along with me: an incredibly tall vet student from England, Joey, a feisty Brazilian girl named Adriana, a group of four Australian newlyweds who mostly kept to themselves, and a beautiful French couple whose names escape me now. They fought constantly, but when they were being pleasant to each other they sure were nice to look at.

The climb itself was brilliant and not too challenging on the first day which consisted of a 2,000-meter climb from Senaru at 600 meters to the crater rim at 2,600 meters. The beginning of the trail wove through something between a jungle and a forest – slightly piney and slightly viney. We got lucky when we stumbled upon a bunch of long, sturdy sticks, and each of us picked one up to use as a walking stick, except for Joey who took two.

Throughout most of the hike I had the trail to myself given we all walked at different speeds and I was somewhere in the middle. Joey advanced far ahead, which I credited to his incredibly long legs and perhaps the two sticks he was using. Adriana walked the slowest, which she insisted was her method and that we shouldn't worry as she would always catch up. She liked her solitude on the hikes and I understood.

We stopped partway up for lunch and the guide spread a blanket on the ground for everyone to sit on, then gave us cookies and tea while we waited for the porters to cook. When the main course came it was a noodle soup with boiled eggs and a pineapple. I thought it was pretty good for a hiking meal and that trend continued throughout the trek.

As we continued onwards and upwards, we left the trees behind and started climbing around yellow and orange rocks. I lost the trail for a moment and had to backtrack but I didn't mind too much. Finally, we made it to the crater and the brilliant view was a great sign of what was to come over the next few days.

The clouds cleared to reveal a volcano within a crater, surrounded by a deep bluish-green water. As the clouds cleared completely we could see the entirety of the lake and it was stunning. I'd never seen water quite that color. To the right, the ocean stretched out endlessly to Bali and beyond.

The sun set as we put up our tents. I had my own as well as a light sleeping bag as both were included in the trekking price. It turned out to be freezing up there, and I was glad that I'd asked the guide if I could borrow a jacket the morning before we started the trek.

I noticed that the more expensive trekking companies brought along chairs and a tent to put around a hole in the ground that served as a bathroom. I was still glad that I didn't pay extra just for those small luxuries. Sitting on the ground and bush toilets don't bother me.

The second day of the trek we woke up with the sun. We were told it was an amazing view, but sadly there was cloud cover and we couldn't see it. That was all right, though, because the views to come would be even more spectacular.

We made a steep descent down to the crater lake surrounding the volcano. The porters and guides did it all in flip-flops while the rest of us struggled not to slip and fall off the narrow rock trail in our running shoes and hiking boots. I couldn't believe the locals were handling it with such ease, but I suppose they owe their agility to experience.

The lake was even more impressive up close. The guides invited us to go for a swim, and after sticking my toe in and finding that it was absolutely freezing, I was leaning towards sitting that one out.

"How often do you get to swim in a volcano crater lake?" asked Adriana. I couldn't argue with that point, so I stripped down to my bathing suit and jumped in with her. I was hot and sweaty from the hike so the temperature wasn't entirely unpleasant after all.

Next we made our way closer to the hot springs which sounded pretty darn good to me in my soaking-wet state at that point. The water was close to 100 degrees in some spots, which were my favorite since I like my water just one step below scalding. The setting was gorgeous: layered pools of water with varying degrees of heat depending on how close we got to the source. Mountains shot up all around, encircling the pools. I wished I could have brought a camera that wouldn't have been ruined by the water. No matter; some things are just better committed to memory.

After lunch, I picked up my clothes and set off to find a rock large enough to change behind. Up until this point, the macaques were content to rummage through the trash left behind by other porters, more or less ignoring we humans. This time, though, one of them decided to take a stand as I walked by.

He came running at me, teeth bared, ready to chomp right into my leg. All in an instant it occurred to me that I never got a rabies shot. I was very far from any kind of help if he did bite me, and there was no way I could outrun him.

For some reason that I still don't quite understand, I decided to bare my teeth right back, scream at the top of my lungs, and raise my arms up as if I was going in for an attack as well. The look on his face went from ferociousness to pure fear and he retreated immediately. Vindicated, I doubled over laughing and when I finally regained composure, continued onward to my rock and changed. Nobody was going to ruin my day, least of all a primate.

We arrived at the base of the Rinjani volcano in the late afternoon to a few touts at the top selling beer and snacks, for a markup, of course. Joey, Adriana, and I thought it was a genius idea and were in full support of these guys hiking up to make the sale and rewarded them with a purchase each. It was an early night that night because the next day would be the most grueling of all.

The final day was by far the toughest but most gorgeous and rewarding. Those of us who wanted to climb the 1,000 meters to the summit, which was about half of the group, woke up at 2am the next morning. We strapped on our headlamps, warm clothing, and watched as the guides put on real shoes for the first time. This was a clear sign that the trail was about to get really difficult.

Given the volcanic gravel, the climb consisted of regularly climbing two steps forward only to slide at least one back. It took about three hours to make it all the way to the top with freezing winds pelting me the whole way. It was a tough mental and physical battle to beat the sunrise. I couldn't rest for too long at any point because then I'd arrive too late at the top and miss the best part of the whole hike as the sun rises over the volcano and sea.

I reached the top with moments to spare, feeling accomplished and ecstatic as the sun rose, illuminating the volcano and the surrounding islands all the way to Bali. Just as I stood on top of Kinabalu in Borneo a couple weeks prior, there I was standing on top of Lombok. I could see Gili Trawangan in the distance, where I'd be heading later that day.

By the time I descended, my shoes were full of about an ounce each of volcanic dust and rubble and the tents had been taken down. It was time to climb all the way back down to the bottom of the volcano and to the other side of the jungle. We somehow beat all of the other groups to the bottom and climbed into a van to return to Senaru so that we could pick up our belongings. From there, we funneled into two different cars. I gave Joey and Adriana hugs goodbye and made my way for the port. Once again, I would take public transport to my next stop.

The van dropped me off and I ignored the touts offering tickets, electing to buy directly from the source inside of the ticketing office for $1. The ferry took about twenty minutes and as I docked at Gili T, I smiled back on the day. It had been a challenge and it had been rewarding.

Now I have grand plans to party and laze on the beach for a while. That's what Gili T is known for, after all.

53

July 12-17, 2013

Days 288 - 293

Uh-oh, I've done it again. I've found a beach town that I can't leave and it's pulling me in.

Now I've been to a lot of pretty nice beaches over the past 10 months and Gili T isn't the best of them all. It's not even close, but what I love about this place is the people I've met here.

John, a gentlemanly English guy from my live-aboard dive boat in Komodo is here, plus Camille, a drop-dead gorgeous brunette from the Faroe Islands with a sense of humor and wit that keeps me on my toes, and Andrew, an Englishman who teaches at an international school in the Philippines and is on summer break. I met him my first night here when, despite the fatigue from the early morning hike, I went out on my veranda hoping to make some friends. He's my neighbor, and it didn't take long for us to strike up a conversation and make plans to hang out the next day.

This group is tons of fun, and each day we grab a few drinks, lie on the sand, and just laugh and talk. We could be anywhere, honestly, but we're here now and it's paradise.

Though this place is a bit touristy, I don't really care at this point. It's not overly debaucherous like Kuta in Bali would be or like so many of the islands in Thailand were, and I can't think of a better way to unwind from the hiking than to spend some time on a nice beach.

Gili T does have some lovely coral sand and that aquamarine water that I've seen throughout so much of Southeast Asia. When it's that color, it might as well be wearing a sign that says, "I'm warm, really warm, don't you want to take a dip?"

For some reason the mosquitoes don't bite as much here. I don't know why, but I'm not looking a gift horse in the mouth, either.

I won't lie – I've been dancing every night away. It's a party island that lives up to its reputation. I've been sleeping in and just enjoying that most of what this small island has to offer is right outside my doorstep. I don't have to go far to enjoy pretty much everything on this tiny island.

'Gili' means 'small island' in Bahasa, and it's a fitting name, indeed.

I was supposed to get on the ferry out yesterday, but I missed it, oops. I was supposed to get on it today too, but the same thing seems to have happened. I promise I'll get on it tomorrow, though.

My time is running out as my flight home is in less than a week. That's right; in less than a week I'll be back in Southern California. I sent my mom a message that read, "I haven't worn shoes all week, haven't worn makeup in months, and haven't worn normal pants in even longer. How do I ever go back to normal life?"

I'm trying not to think about that too much.

54

July 18, 2013

Day 294

I think maybe I should have just stayed on Gili Trawangan.

Traveling is usually meant to be a vacation, a departure from stress and difficulties, and an overall pleasant experience. But sometimes, traveling absolutely, positively, unavoidably, goes horribly wrong, and yesterday, traveling really sucked for me.

I saw dead people.

To rewind to the beginning, I took a speedboat out of Gili T bound for Bali in the early morning. Well, it was supposed to be the early morning but it was delayed for about an hour, because that's just how Southeast Asia is sometimes. That's okay, I'm used to it now.

While I waited I saw a small fisherman's boat come and pick up a few kids with backpacks. I guess that's the school bus system in the Gilis (there are two other islands, Meno and Air), and it was cool to see it.

There is a smaller, local boat that also heads to Bali but it takes almost three times as long, and I'm running out of time. I did, however, elect to go local for the rest of the trip.

The boat pulled up to Bali and most of the tourists got in

vans to go elsewhere – Kuta, Ubud, or Sanur. I made my way to a bus station in Denpasar, jumping off the van before the rest of the tourists who were heading to the airport. It was a ghost town which isn't what I expected. I bargained with an ojek driver who took me to another station where I caught a bus that would eventually take me across Bali, over the sea via ferry, and onwards to Java.

Adriana, my hiking buddy from Rinjani, had shown me photos of blazing blue flames at another volcano called Kawah Ijen. She raved that it was one of the best parts of her trip so I elected to bypass Bali so that I could see them with my own eyes, too.

I settled into the bus after waving off the touts and once again paying for the ticket inside. It was a few dollars. I was happy to look out the window and just enjoy the ride.

Once again, I was the only foreigner onboard. It was sparsely filled. I saw a mother pour cough syrup into a spoon and force-feed it to her baby. She looked up at me and winked after. Should I have been concerned? It did mean we'd at least have a quiet ride, or so I thought.

Guitar players got on every now and then to play songs and solicit tips. I sometimes gave some change and sometimes I didn't. It depended on how good they were. I looked out the window and regretted that I didn't have more time to explore Bali, too. The Hindu culture there, in contrast to the Muslim and sometimes Christian cultures elsewhere in the country, resulted in quite intricate and unique architecture that stood out from the rest of the country.

Pretty soon we came to a stop and I looked out the window to see that we were crawling thanks to gridlock.

"Wow," I thought, "Bali has some seriously bad traffic."

After the bus had been at a complete standstill for nearly half an hour I started to worry. There was some discussion between the locals, but, not speaking Bahasa I shrugged and trusted that eventually someone would try to communicate with me if I needed to know what was going on. I've found that there's always someone kind enough to try.

Eventually everyone on the bus stood up and looked toward the window. I only had to turn my head slightly to see why we had been stopped for so long – a policeman pulled a shroud off the face of a departed motorbiker on the side of the road just as we passed. A chill ran down my spine. I thought of my motorbike crash that I had survived, unscathed, in Sumatra and counted my blessings.

The bus broke down a few more times before getting stuck in another long line of traffic. This time, it was a large truck that had veered off the road, smashing the cabin entirely and creating another two-hour backup. Crowds of locals surrounded it as we passed. Another chill went down my spine – there's no way, judging by the cab, that the driver made it out alive.

There we were, eight hours into what was meant to be a four-hour journey from Bali to Java, and we had at least another three to go.

The bus broke down again.

This time, we were ordered off, passed up by a few more buses, and then ordered back on when a local mechanic had jerry-rigged a solution.

When we finally got to the ferry terminal it was dark and so far behind schedule that I wondered what time I'd finally get to Banuwagi, one of the jumping-off points for the volcano.

The ferry docked in Java, and I climbed back on the bus. We had picked up some stragglers on board and suddenly the cabin was crawling with cockroaches.

Now, I don't mind snakes. I don't even mind spiders. Most insects are just fine with me, but I cannot handle cockroaches. I have a physical repulsion to them. I know that they can't hurt me but it's the very concept of their disgusting, crap-eating existence that I just can't handle. The ride had gone from bad to worse.

We pulled up to Banyuwagi at 3 AM. I thought that's where I wanted to head, but judging by the look of the town and the fact that I didn't want to be dropped off in the middle of nowhere at 3 AM, I checked the suggestions I had written down from Laura and asked if the bus was going to Bondowoso.

Sure, the attendant nodded, it was.

The sun rose as the bus docked at a terminal and I was told that was the end of the line. I was the only one left on the bus and I had felt for a while that the other shoe was probably going to drop. It was not Bondowoso, though, that was for sure.

The attendant came up to me and said, "Vroom vroom! Harley-Davidson!" and I just looked at him blankly. He pointed out the window and I realized he meant I was going to have to get on an ojek. A man was waiting there for me, an extra helmet in his hand.

"What's this going to cost?" I asked.

"Up to you," he replied.

It was an odd answer, but I was in no position to negotiate and nearly delirious from the lack of sleep and food.

He brought me to his house where his wife didn't make eye contact even after I greeted her and wished her a good morning in Bahasa. His children stole glances at me from the next room as they watched a dubbed version of *Spongebob Squarepants* and I sat on a mat in the entrance room, wondering how the hell I had gotten into this situation.

Finally he reappeared from another room in the home.

"I'm sorry, I really don't understand," I pleaded.

He ushered me back to another motorbike and said, "cousin," handing me a helmet and passing me onto another stranger. It was time to go.

I've been on many motorbikes before at this point, but this guy really drove like a bat out of hell, weaving in and out of traffic like a madman. Trying to forget the scenes from the side of the road the day before in Bali. I was a complete mute, powerless to say anything.

We jetted past several odd sights including a man carrying a ten-foot pole on his motorbike, an overstuffed motorbike with toys and bright plastic buckets, and a motorbike with a teenage passenger carrying an uncovered chain saw. Yes, an uncovered chainsaw, because the day couldn't have gotten any stranger or worse.

Hours later we reached the park entrance for Kawah Ijen where I was illegally charged $2 by the attendant and led to a guesthouse that I hadn't asked for.

I'd read horrible reviews about the place and I knew I wanted to bypass it. Eventually I convinced them that no, I would not be paying USD $20 to stay in this shithole and could he please take me where I had asked to go in Bondowoso? He brought me to his brother's house a few streets over instead. He showed me a water-stained room with a disgusting-looking bed and an obvious insect problem and said it would cost $15 to stay there.

"I just want to go here, this is too expensive," I kept repeating, showing him on the map.

"Where you from?" he asked.

"Why does that matter?" I replied, a bit of venom in my voice at this point.

I knew it wasn't out of fascination like it normally is in Indonesia. The timing of it just didn't make sense. He kept acting like an American should have no problem paying the asking price to stay there.

"Take me back to Bondowoso, then," I insisted, which they of course tried to talk me out of.

I was finally tired of being walked all over. After 24 hours of no sleep and hardly any food it was all I could do to keep from losing face. I put my foot down and calmly insisted that they take me back down the mountain. They finally relented.

The ride back consisted of almost crashing into a family on bikes, stopping at the driver's home for whatever inconceivable reason while I tried to be friendly but almost lost it waiting for him to change jackets, and lots of bumpy, steep roads.

When I finally arrived at the dirty hotel I'd asked for, since it was the only one I could find when I was researching, I threw down my bag, politely ushered the driver away, positively shocked that he accepted $10 for the hours of driving, as I was sure he'd try to ask for an astronomical amount, and finally collapsed onto the bed.

The room smelled of cigarettes and the hotel was eerily silent. I emerged looking for food but since it's Ramadan right now and all the restaurants are closed, I could only find junk food at a convenience store across the street. I accepted it, ate some cookies and crackers, then fell into a deep sleep.

Java, I'm not sure about you yet, but I'm going to try to give you a chance. So far this has been my worst day of travel yet.

55

July 19, 2013

Day 295

I awoke groggy this morning and had a breakfast of crackers with fake cheese on them.

I don't even like cheese, much less fake cheese, but I was determined to have a better day after asking sending a message to Adriana, asking her advice on how to do Kawah Ijen independently. Almost everyone who climbs the volcano books a tour, but I've found the tour companies in Southeast Asia to be one big scam, stopping at tourist traps expecting us to buy trinkets and generally making things take hours longer and cost double what they need to. That's not for me.

I knew there was a public bus and asked around at my guesthouse for the departure time. I was told 7 AM, 9 AM, and 10 AM. Like traveling elsewhere in Indonesia, departure time probably just varies. I arrived at 9am and waited for only 20 minutes. As soon as I pulled up in the bicycle tuk-tuk at the bus station, just a few minutes away from the guesthouse I'd stayed in, everyone knew exactly why I was there and pointed me to the correct bus. How nice of them.

The ride up took around 2.5 hours as it made frequent stops for supplies. When we turned into the entrance of the park,

I ducked this time, not letting the guards see me and charge me another fake entrance fee. It worked, and we were waved through.

The cost of the bus was 35,000 rupiah, which I thought was a ripoff until running into a fellow independent traveler later that day who was charged 50,000 for the same ride the day before. I'm guessing the locals paid about a quarter of what I paid.

After the drop-off point I turned left down the road from the bus stop in Sempol and walked the 1km to Arabica Guesthouse thanks to the sign advertising its location. This was the same place that wanted $20 from me the day before, but Laura confirmed it was the only place in town to stay at so I reluctantly went back. When I showed up, they said they were fully booked. That was a curveball I didn't expect.

I trudged back down the road, sweating profusely and cursing the past 48 hours. I really missed Gili T at that point. Just when I was about to give up hope, I spotted another foreigner coming my way. We met halfway on the road and I couldn't believe my luck. It turned out he was also an American guy from Colorado. He also trekked Kawah Ijen without a tour and he was on his way to check out of the guesthouse I had just walked out of. I asked him if I could walk back with him and try to get his room. He said, "Of course!"

We approached the counter again together and the woman who had dismissively waved me off before was suddenly warm and smiling, replying that of course I could have his room. It would be no problem. She quoted me $18, and he quickly said, "but I only paid $15," so she relented.

"Okay, $15. Follow me."

She led me to a room that was clearly not the boy's from Colorado and was about as disappointing as the one I stayed in the night before. It was moderately clean and moderately dirty at the same time. It had an ensuite bathroom and two beds. Whatever, I was just happy to have somewhere to stay.

I thanked Colorado guy and bid him goodbye as he headed back for the bus stop. Later that night, disinterested in paying Western prices for iffy food, I walked to a small eatery called a warung that I'd seen on my walk in. On my way, teenage boys pulled up on a motorbike and made rude gestures at me. I made a rude one right back with my middle finger and offered some choice words. They drove away.

I am completely out of patience with this place and very glad that it wasn't my first stop of my journey or I might have booked a ticket back home and ugly-cried the whole way.

Luckily the woman at the warung was kind and gentle, and she had my favorite Indonesian food, tempeh, which is whole soybeans pressed into a cake and sautéed with cashews and basil. A good meal has a way of turning my mood right around, and I felt happy again.

I returned to the guesthouse, and as I walked a gorgeous sunset unfolded behind the mountains and trees. I took a few deep breaths in and finally felt calm. It's only 8 PM but it's my bedtime now since an ojek is coming to pick me up around 2 AM to start the hike into the crater with the stars. I think this just might finally work out.

56

July 20, 2013 (Morning)

Day 296

Adriana was so right. The blue flames were spectacular, and this was definitely a highlight of my trip so far!

The ojek driver thankfully showed up as planned and drove for about 15 minutes to the start of the trail. Several gentlemen were waiting there to offer guide services but I told them I was just fine on my own, headlamp in hand and sarong wrapped around my shoulders for warmth.

Hiking in with the stars made it a really beautiful experience. The initial three kilometers or so were steep but it evened out after that. Eventually I caught up to a French guy, the only other person on the trail at that hour, who was also hiking on his own and we reached the crater rim together, laying eyes on the royal blue flames for the first time.

They seemed surreal. I'd seen Adriana's photos but nothing could prepare me for what the flames looked like in person.

A local sulfur miner walked up and offered to show us the way down. We accepted knowing we'd have to give him a tip, but it seemed like a better way to experience the flames up close.

The sulfur miners are tough as nails. They carry as much

as 200 pounds of sulfur transported in two baskets with a wooden plank in between, up and down the 3,000-foot crater all day and night. They're only paid around $1 per 30 pounds and I noticed that most of them clearly had severe spinal issues, not to mention the toxic fumes they constantly breathe in.

They happily posed for photos, some of them asking for a tip in return and others just happy for the moment of fame. Others take the sulfur and carve it into little yellow turtles and other shapes to sell to tourists coming by. They can sell these little trinkets for more than they can make by carrying the sulfur, but most appear to do both.

Our impromptu guide brought us directly, and dangerously, close to the flames. Every now and then the winds would change and send the toxic fumes right toward us, burning my eyes and cutting off all air sources. I covered my face with my sarong and ducked behind a rock.

Jerome, the French guy, and I agreed that this would never be allowed back home, but it was pretty cool to get so close right then and there, asphyxiating fumes and all.

After about ten minutes we couldn't take the fumes anymore and hiked back up to the crater rim to wait for the sunrise. It turns out Jerome, slightly shorter than I am and sporting glasses and shaggy brown hair, is an eye doctor who is on a two-week holiday. He was fascinated that I've been traveling for so long solo and our conversation quickly turned interesting and stimulating, though the sun rising just over the crater interrupted us and stole all of our attention.

This is easily one of the most incredible sunrises I've seen. I thought back to the sunrise in Haad Rin on the morning of my 27th birthday and thought, "these two could battle it out for domination."

The sky seemed to change colors in layers. First it was blue, then pink, then orange, and then yellow. I could see the sulfur down below, a brilliant yellow in contrast to the blue-green lake in the crater. There were so many colors that it looked like someone had taken a paintbrush and filled it all in strictly according to his imagination – full of fantasy and pixie dust.

Upon climbing back down, the masses of tour groups passed us by and I couldn't believe that they had missed out on the flames and the sunrise. It seems pointless to me to head to Ijen and not try to see the flames. Once the sun is up, you can't see them anymore. Save for a couple other tourists, Jerome and I had the sunrise vista and the blue flames all to ourselves.

Once we reached the bottom it was time to part ways. I was getting on an ojek to head back and get some sleep, and Jerome was bound for Bromo via Jeep where I'd be heading later in the afternoon via public bus.

"I like to take portraits of people I've met on my journey, would you mind?" he asked, holding up his DSLR camera.

There were bags under my eyes, my hair was in disarray, and I was wrapped in dirty clothes and a beat-up sarong, but I stood and smiled, because why not?

We didn't trade contact information because sometimes you just appreciate the moment for what it is then and there, and you know that you'll never see each other again, and that's all right.

As I sit here on the bed in my guesthouse, I don't really mind that it's too expensive or not clean enough, because today was a good day, and it's only 9 AM. Time for some sleep, guys, I'll catch you later.

57

July 20, 2013 (Evening)

It had been a tiring day. It was take two of my attempt at climbing Kawah Ijen, and I had woken up at 1 AM in order to see the stars and blue flames. I was on cloud nine but quickly crashed back to reality when I realized I'd have to go face another battle at the bus stop later.

Sure enough, several young men rode by taunting me, making rude and suggestive gestures, but I just ignored them this time and kept my nose in my book. I really had no idea how long I'd have to wait for the bus, or if it would even come, as nobody had much of a clue as to the time it would arrive. I think per usual in Indonesia, it just comes when it comes. I settled in for a long wait.

Then something odd happened. A truck carrying a brand-new motorbike pulled over and a uniformed young man stepped out.

"Bondowoso?" he asked.

Yes, that was where I was going. I needed to get to the bus depot so that I could catch another bus onwards toward Mt. Bromo, the final stop of my trip.

He offered me a ride. Skeptical and jaded, I asked how much money he was looking for. He looked surprised and a little wounded and said he wanted nothing. Something about his demeanor made me trust him, and I climbed inside with him and his two coworkers.

Before long, we were joking around and I was speaking with them in my very limited Bahasa, which I've picked up between Malaysia and Indonesia over the combined previous three months while they did the same in their very limited English. We even stopped by a grocery store and they told me I could wait in the car. They emerged with a cold drink for me and the driver even though they, given it was Ramadan, had to abstain.

How sweet is that?

We dropped off the motorbike and they invited me into the buyer's lovely home. Everyone was incredibly kind and I eventually made it to the bus station safe and sound. Just as promised, they wanted nothing from me. They drove away, waving as they went, and I pinched myself. I couldn't believe what had just happened and though I didn't understand why they were so kind. I felt so grateful.

I wish I could tell them now how much that really meant to me. It was one simple act of kindness but it set the tone for the rest of the day's trip, which ended up being a little easier, maybe simply due to my more positive outlook.

They say all it takes to ruin a place is one bad egg, but I think the opposite. All it took to restore my faith in Java was one random act of kindness.

58

July 21-23, 2013

Days 297-299

Mount Bromo is probably Indonesia's most famous volcano. It sits at the eastern end of Java between Surabaya and Yogyakarta and is quite often lumped in as part of a tour heading out of one of those two cities which usually includes Kawah Ijen, the volcano I'd just been to.

After the incredibly kind gentlemen dropped me off at the public bus station in Bondowoso, I hopped on a bus bound for Probolinggo that left just 20 minutes later. My timing was good. The price was right, too, and I only paid 16,000 rupiah (USD $1.60) to the bus attendant and settled in for the four-hour ride. Naturally, we stopped a few times to let on guitar-playing buskers and snack touts.

The ride took me through absolutely stunning countryside full of coconut palms and rolling green hills. We'd left the rice paddies behind on the other islands but Java, or at least the eastern part, has its own special beauty. The sunset was incredible, dipping below the trees and painting everything gold as we wove through the forested hills.

I'd read that from Probolinggo, a small bus takes off for Cemoro Lawang, the base of Bromo, when full. I alighted from the bigger bus I'd taken from Bondowoso and walked around the big bus station a bit, finally finding a little kiosk that sold tickets for the smaller mini-bus to Cemoro Lawang.

It was well after dark by the time we pulled into the little town. I'd made friends with a young, newly married couple on our way in and we decided to work together to find an appropriate guesthouse. We asked the driver to take us as close to the starting point of the hike to Bromo as possible, and he obliged. There was a little homestay right there and the price was right, so we took the only two rooms they had.

The next morning we made the leisurely walk to the Bromo volcano crater which is a mostly flat walk across a sand sea, bypassing a Hindu temple nestled within the sand dunes. I could see tire tracks from the Jeeps and was glad that we set out in the afternoon, well after they'd already taken the tourists through earlier in the day. We climbed up a set of stairs to the crater opening and peered over the edge. It was smoking like crazy and undoubtedly still quite active.

Out of the corner of my eye I noticed a little Indonesian girl on the viewing platform who was beside herself with excitement. I really didn't understand why until she bounded over to me and her father motioned with his camera, asking to take a photo. I nodded and communicated that I wanted a photo too. It was the cutest interaction and I wonder if perhaps she thought I was someone famous. I don't even know if there's such a thing as an F-list but if so, I think I'm firmly on it.

I spent the rest of the afternoon in a local warung getting to know the couple better. The guy moved to the Netherlands from Canada for a gap year and they'd met at a hostel he worked at and got married so that they could always live in the same place without worrying about visas. Sometimes it seems to me that these marriages are more for convenience than anything but in this case I could tell it was for love.

The next day at 3:30 AM, jacket on that I'd rented from a guesthouse across the road, hand-drawn map in hand, and headlamp in tow, I started what turned out to be about a two-hour climb. The path was pretty obvious for the most part until I got past the first viewing platform and it turned a bit muddy and treacherous. My new friends stayed behind as their knees were bothering them, but I simply had to make it to the top to see what the fuss was about.

It wasn't nearly as challenging as Rinjani or Kinabalu but was a great way to get some exercise and avoid crowds of people – 99% of whom took Jeeps up to the top rather than their feet.

The summit itself was so full of cars and people that I was instantly turned off. The hordes of other tourists made it almost impossible to get a decent view, so I climbed through the railings and stood with the bushes in front so that I could catch a glimpse. The volcano rose up over a sea of clouds that floated in the crater and the little town of Cemoro Lawang glittered to the left of it. More volcanoes and mountains became visible behind Bromo as the sun rose ever higher. I understood right then why Bromo is so popular – it's stunning.

The benefit of not being on a tour was that I could wait for the crowds to clear out after the sunrise to get some more decent pictures. Those on a tour didn't have the luxury of waiting around for a clearer vista nor did they get the satisfaction of climbing to the top.

I walked back down and met up with my friends on the way. They'd enjoyed the sunrise as well from their little viewpoint and it seemed that there was no wrong way to view it in the end.

For a final stop on my Southeast Asia and a little bit Oceania tour, I was happy to have spent it watching the day begin over Mt. Bromo.

59

July 24, 2013

Day 300

As I watch the sun set on the final day of my travels I can't help but smile to myself. I'm coming into the last day of my trip the same way I came into the first day and approached my travels from the beginning: solo.

From the 7th floor of a hotel in Surabaya, Java, I look out on rooftops, listen to the mosque as it announces sundown since we're in the middle of Ramadan, and reflect on my decision to take off on this open-ended trip almost exactly ten months ago.

It feels like so long ago now that I was searching for flights, fighting clammy hands and a fast-beating heart as I clicked 'confirm' on my one-way ticket to Bangkok, then tried to combat the fear of the unknown. So much has changed since then.

I could have never expected the things that happened this year to take my life in the direction it has taken, could never have guessed how many people I'd meet who would change my point of view and my entire trajectory, and had no idea that it would all lead me to where I am now, so very thankful for the moment.

Remember? It all started in Bangkok when I nervously stepped off that plane and really hit its stride in Siem Reap when I met an amazing group of fellow solo travelers at my hostel who I spent the rest of my time with in that amazing town, biking around Angkor Wat and realizing that, yes, solo travel is actually an extremely social way to travel, after all.

I realized that it wouldn't be so hard; I wouldn't be alone much after all. Maybe I had been so scared for so long for absolutely no reason.

I fell so hard in love with Cambodia that by the time I left, my heart hurt and I knew I had left a piece of myself behind there, right with the smiling children who chased after me laughing and yelling hello.

Laos taught me that I could jump on a (scary, scary) motorbike and have an adventure. The natural beauty astounded me and I still tell people it's my favorite country I've visited so far.

Thailand brought a new set of life changes that I never in a million years thought would come. I got my first tattoo, and I let a monk pick it out for me. Even crazier, I actually canceled my booking for the full moon party on New Year's Eve and spent it in silence meditating at a Buddhist wat.

Australia taught me about following love and losing it, only to fall in love with travel again. Everything happens for a reason and I see that now.

Malaysia brought me back to the roots of travel – hanging out with locals and experiencing previously unimaginable hospitality. I'm so glad I didn't listen to anyone who said Malaysia wasn't worth spending time in. They were simply wrong.

Indonesia has proved to be the most challenging yet most rewarding country yet that I've traversed solo and independently. It pushed me to take my patience and persistence to a new level.

It all began with a half-baked dream back in a grey cubicle, a whole lot of self-doubt, and a healthy dose of fear. There were a lot of ardent supporters who I will always be grateful for, and a few naysayers who I'll always be glad I didn't listen to.

The most surprising thing about all of this is that I'm still unsure and scared. I'm scared every day, but not of traveling anymore. I'm scared of what happens if it ends. Each time someone asks, "What will you do when you're done traveling?" I shudder a little bit. That is the one question that, from the beginning, I never had an answer to.

"It will come to me on the road," I always said.

As I close this chapter of life, wandering, thousands of hellos and an equally high number of goodbyes, new friends, new beginnings, hundreds of brilliant sunsets and awe-inspiring sunrises, hours of laughter, times of frustration, jar after jar of Tiger Balm to soothe the mosquito bites, mental calculations of baht, Dong, rupiah, kip, riel, and ringgit, countless random acts of kindness and thousands of smiles, my heart feels heavy with nostalgia, warmth for the good times, a little bit of pain, a whole lot of love, and even more anxious anticipation of what's to come.

Most of all, I just feel grateful. I feel grateful for everything that happened, even if it seemed frustrating or heartbreaking at the time. When I look back on it now, even the things that seemed like they were taking me backwards were really pushing me forward, and that's how I've come to realize life is.

It's about trusting in the journey and fully surrendering to it, knowing that the steps that I'm taking right now are bringing me to where I'm meant to be eventually. Even this moment, one day, as I sit here unsure of what's to come, will be poignant and pleasing to think back on.

The only thing that is clear to me right now is that my wandering isn't finished. It can't be. I'm not ready.

I've missed everyone from California, and it's still home, so when I say this, please don't get me wrong:

I'm coming home, but I have a plan.

I won't be staying for too long.

Epilogue

The fan slows before coming to a stop in the bamboo bungalow I've rented for the week in Tofo, Mozambique. Outside I can hear the waves rolling in softly, just as they did last night when they soothed me to sleep. The beach here is long and flat and when the tide comes in, it forms long pools in the sand, reflecting the sky like giant mirrors. The big, fluffy clouds often come to play as well, just to add a little something for the sun to reflect on when it sets in the sky.

It's 10am and the power has just gone out. I try to roll over and carry on sleeping but my stomach protests that it's time for my daily 10-cent coconut. I take it as a sign to finally open my eyes and greet the day. It's warm in my room and I know it's the right thing to do to make my way outside into the breeze.

I push aside the mosquito net and elect not to bother with brushing my hair. I haven't done it all week and see no good reason to start now. I don't bother with shoes either, mainly because I don't know where I left them. I play a game of "where are my shoes?" almost daily. I always find them, though, so I'm not worried. Surely they're around here somewhere.

I make a beeline for the set of three hammocks near the open-air kitchen. They face the ocean and I've been logging some serious time in there in between taking swigs of Dois M beer and telling jokes with my new group of friends. Every now and then we find some motivation and go for swims in the cool blue water and head over to the point at the end of the beach for the sunsets.

I love these guys. They treat me like a member of the guy crew and it reminds me of the camaraderie from my bike gang in Siem Reap and my girl crew in Pai. My goodness, that was two years ago now!

It's November 2015 and I have a couple of weeks left in Mozambique. It's a coastal country in Southern Africa, which has quickly become my new favorite part of the world. As soon as I checked my phone this morning I noticed that another article has gone up on *Business Insider* talking about how I left my old job to build a life as a travel writer and photographer.

This comes on the heels of a few other major media articles that have come out lately. It seemed to come in a huge wave after I wrote my guidebook and I'm so happy that what started out as a dream has morphed into a career. Thanks to all of this I'm feeling particularly nostalgic today and reflect on the series of wild adventures, new discoveries, old heartbreaks, and unfamiliar horizons I've seen since those early days in Southeast Asia.

When I said I had a plan at the end of my last post of my first year of traveling, it was a bold statement for a writer whose ventures weren't profitable yet. Then I started to get a few modest freelance roles that kept me afloat while my audience grew. Sometimes I spent weeks on end, 14 hours per day, seven days per week, at my computer fighting to be heard, learning all I could, and tirelessly chasing a dream of retaining my nomadic status.

During this time I read a lot of books about human

psychology and Buddhism in order to reconcile the alone time and to understand the inner workings of my mind better. I went through extreme ups and extreme downs but came out appreciating each one for what it did for me. They all helped me to grow and this has been as much a voyage of world discovery as it has been a voyage of self-discovery.

There were times when I wondered if this lifestyle was worth it. There were a lot of moments when I questioned if it was too isolating, if it only fostered short and meaningless relationships, or if I was shooting myself in the foot by giving up stability for uncertainty. I wondered if I was being selfish or immature.

Then, a random stranger would pick me up from the side of the road and drive me for hundreds of miles for free, a local would invite me to a meal with his family, or I'd make it to the summit of another mountain, and I'd realize that this ride is magical, beautiful, and so worthwhile. For all of the sacrifices, there is an equal measure of little pleasures. Beyond the places I went and the professional wins, I learned one of the most important takeaways of all – I am loved and supported by a lot of amazing people and I am not done exploring yet.

Over the past two years I fell in love in Dublin, which carried over to the Maldives and Sri Lanka where I fell out of it again, I traveled through the Philippines and Vietnam to finish off my Southeast Asia travels, hitchhiked solo through two provinces in China, climbed to over 18,000 feet in Nepal on my 28th birthday, was granted residency in Berlin, Germany, trekked in the Alps through four countries, got a few more tattoos, attended Burning Man a couple more times, traveled solo through South Africa for nearly three months and it became my favorite country, went all through the surrounding countries in the month that followed, sleeping in a tent the whole way through, confronted my fear of winter in the Arctic in January, and learned to ski in Austria.

When I think back on the girl in the cubicle, the one who was told that she couldn't ever be happy anywhere if she couldn't be happy with that life she held back then, I'm so glad that she took a leap of faith and didn't listen to the naysayers. Rather than acting out of fear and holding onto a life that didn't feel right, I acted out of love for myself and curiosity for the world and took a chance. I hope that any woman who finds herself in that position does the same.

I've had crazy adventures since that I've never breathed a word about to anyone, and my brain and heart are bursting with beautiful memories – so many that it will take years to tell them all, which I aim to do. There is so much to say and I could fill pages forever with the chance encounters, small miracles, incredible kindness of strangers, beautiful sunrises and sunsets, eureka! moments, long hugs, deep and meaningful conversations, and terrifying situations that all ended up all right.

My heart is bursting at the seams, and there's a whole world of people who have impacted me in beautiful ways. I could never have imagined all of the experiences I would have thanks to pushing the 'purchase' button for that one-way flight to Bangkok over three years ago now.

But all that is a story for another time.

About the Author

Kristin Addis is the solo female traveler behind BeMyTravelMuse.com, a website for off-the-beaten-path adventures. For the past three years, she's traveled the world alone, hitchhiking in China, sleeping in a tent for over a month in Africa, and learning how to say 'I love you' in 12 Asian languages. She was selected by *USA Today* as a top vagabonding blogger and has been featured in Trip Advisor for Business, Lonely Planet, and BuzzFeed, among others. If you're a girl who is dying to travel the world on your own but don't know where to begin, read the guidebook for solo female travelers: *Conquering Mountains, How to Solo Travel the World Fearlessly*, so that you can be changed forever.

Thought Catalog, it's a website.
www.thoughtcatalog.com

Social
facebook.com/thoughtcatalog
twitter.com/thoughtcatalog
tumblr.com/thoughtcatalog
instagram.com/thoughtcatalog

Corporate
www.thought.is

Made in the USA
Lexington, KY
18 October 2017